LIFE IS HUGE!

OTHER BOOKS BY SUSAN JEFFERS, Ph.D.

(in alphabetical order)

Dare to Connect: Reaching out in romance, friendship and the workplace*

Embracing Uncertainty: Achieving peace of mind as we face the unknown*

End the Struggle and Dance with Life: How to build yourself up when the world gets you down*

Feel the Fear . . . and Beyond: Dynamic techniques for doing it anyway*

Feel the Fear and Do It Anyway: How to turn your fear and indecision into confidence and action*

Feel the Fear Power Planner: 90 days to a fuller life

I'm Okay . . . You're a Brat: Setting the priorities straight and freeing you from the guilt and mad myths of parenthood*

Inner Talk for a Confident Day, *Inner Talk for a Love That Works*, *Inner Talk for Peace of Mind* (the Fear-less series)

Losing a Love . . . Finding a Life: Healing the pain of a broken relationship

Opening Our Hearts to Men: Taking charge of our lives and creating a love that works*

The Feel the Fear Guide to Lasting Love

The Little Book of Confidence

The Little Book of Peace of Mind

*Thoughts of Power and Love** (quotes by Susan Jeffers)

---

*Also available in audiotape

AUDIOTAPES FROM LIVE APPEARANCES:

The Art of Fearbusting
A Fearbusting Workshop
Flirting From the Heart
Opening Our Hearts to Each Other

www.susanjeffers.com

LIFE IS HUGE!

Laughing, Loving and Learning from it All

THE WIT AND WISDOM OF

SUSAN JEFFERS

Jeffers
press

A Jeffers Press Book

Copyright © 2004 by Susan Jeffers, Ph.D.

www.jefferspress.com

ISBN: 0-9745776-7-7
Library of Congress Control Number: 2004118302

Publisher's Cataloging-in-Publication
(Provided by Quality Books, Inc.)

Jeffers, Susan J.
Life is huge! : laughing, loving and learning from it all / the wit and wisdom of Susan Jeffers. — 1st Jeffers Press ed.
p. cm.
Originally published: London : Hodder Mobius, 2004.
ISBN 0-9745776-7-7

1. Life. 2. Self-actualization (Psychology) 3. Self improvement.
I. Title.

BD431.J44 2005   128
QBI04-800132

Printed in the USA

This book was originally published in the United Kingdom by Hodder and Stoughton, a division of Hodder Headline.

First Jeffers Press edition published 2005

Book Text Design by Dotti Albertine

DEDICATION

To my wonderful husband.

Mark Shelmerdine,

who fills every day of my life with

a HUGE amount of love.

I am truly blessed.

Nothing is less real than realism.

Details are confusing. It is only by selection,

by elimination, by emphasis

that we get at the real meaning of things.

— Georgia O'Keeffe —

CONTENTS

CONTENTS

ACKNOWLEDGMENTS

My life is definitely HUGE when it comes to all the wonderful people in it. These include the following who, professionally and personally, provided me with incredible support for this book . . . each in their own way.

Dominick Abel, my agent, who has made it possible for my books to be published in more than 100 countries and over 35 languages. Wow!

Tom and SueEllen Strapp of Powersource, who have created www.susanjeffers.com, a very happy and successful website. They make it fun!

The many people around the world, who have let me know in so many ways that I have made a difference in their lives. They can give me no greater gift than that.

My dear friends: Rosanne Yaman, who gave me permission to include the e-mail she sent to her loved ones on September 11, 2001 in the article, "Am I Dreaming?"; Caren and Dick Lobo, long-time friends who have supported my work in so many ways . . . especially through their warm and welcoming bookstore, The Sarasota News and Books; Sir Ken and Lady Terry Robinson, who constantly offer love, support and laughter as we share our dreams; Diana Von Welanetz Wentworth and Ted Wentworth, who offer so many ideas and words of encouragement; Gerald Rafferty, Ph.D., who has given me many valuable suggestions relative to a number of projects; Donna Gradstein, who was my co-writer of our book for children, *I Can Handle It*. She is the "Donna" who appears in a number of the enclosed articles; DC Walton, who offers constant encouragement and valuable feedback.

And the rest of the "gang": Paul Huson, Bill Bast, Lois Luger, Henry Gradstein, Melissa Oberon, John Levoff, Jenny Blackton, Ed Philhower, David Osterlund, Larry Gershman, Trevor Chenery, Sue Chenery, Rosie Bunting, Paula Berenstein, Fiona Copeland, Stewart Copeland, Joy Starr and Mandi Robbins, who continue to love and support me, each in their own way.

My wonderful family: Gerry Gershman, my loving son, who contributed the very moving article, "A Fateful Day"; Leslie Wandmacher and Michael Wandmacher, my loving daughter and son-in-law; my step-children, Anthony Shelmerdine and Alice Shelmerdine, (Anthony is my hero as he broke tradition and took his wife's name!) and Guy Shelmerdine and my new daughter-in-law, Ashley Jacobs. A special thank you to Ashley, who also gave me permission to use her moving September 11th email in the article, "Am I Dreaming?"; and as always, my very special sister, Marcia and brother-in-law, Bruce Rabiner, who I love so dearly.

And most importantly, my husband, Mark Shelmerdine, who supports me in everything I do. My love for him grows . . . and grows . . . and grows.

INTRODUCTION
The Huge-Ness of It All!

Life truly is huge.

> *It is filled with so many emotions* . . . joy, sadness, silliness, seriousness, love, hate, anger, fear, confidence, confusion, curiosity, clarity, courage, calm, panic, peace, happiness . . . and so much more.

> *It is filled with a massive array of experiences that involve* . . . relationships, parenthood, single-hood, career, travel, friendships, alone time, holidays, health, sports, politics, television, war, peace . . . and so much more.

No question about it . . . life truly is huge!

Over the past few years, I have attempted to capture some of the "huge-ness" of life in a monthly column on my website (www.susanjeffers.com). I named this column THE WORLD ACCORDING TO SUSAN JEFFERS as it represents a compilation of personal observations I have collected over time . . . much humor that is a constant necessity in my life . . . important lessons I have learned that I want to pass along to you . . . poignant moments that make me stop and reflect on the purpose of it all . . . and the gift of love that helps me transcend all that is difficult in this world.

These 50 articles vary widely in terms of content and style. The very humorous articles were written long before my first book, *Feel the Fear And Do It Anyway*, was published. The "how to" articles are drawn from a number of my books and are filled with tools for handling important areas of your life. Some of the remaining articles capture a particular moment in time while others reflect my personal feelings about life and the human condition.

It is my hope that the enclosed will entertain you, make you think, make you laugh, make you cry, make you reach out . . . and much more. You may disagree with my sentiments on a number of issues. That is good! In the huge-ness of life, different people hold differing views of it all, which certainly makes life more interesting. As always, I ask that you *take what works for you and let the rest go.* In fact, that's a great rule to use throughout your journey through life.

As I began putting this book together, I considered arranging the articles in terms of subject matter but, with a few exceptions, I decided to present them in a more random fashion. I figured that it would be more interesting for you to read them this way. *Like life itself . . . you never know what's coming next!* You will notice that my signature themes of power, love and connection run through the content of many of the articles even though the subject matter is quite broad. Yes, life is huge, but a healthy sense of power, love and connection certainly underlie the best of what life has to offer.

All the essays stand on their own. If they relate to subject matter discussed in one of my books, I refer you accordingly so that you can explore the topic more deeply. Early in my writing career, I would have been too sheepishly coy to do this; I wouldn't have wanted you to think I was being too pushy! But now pointing you in the right direction seems like the caring thing to do. I say this because beautiful people from all over the world are constantly reminding me that my books are helping them greatly improve their lives. (Thank you, beautiful people!) Therefore, I felt I would be remiss by *not* providing these references.

How do you read this book? That depends on you. You can move through it from beginning to end. Or you can open the book at any point and be surprised at what you may find. Or you can look at the contents and pick the titles that "speak" to you at any given moment. Or you can skip any subject matter that doesn't appeal to you. (On second thought, these may be just the articles you need to read!) In addition to a few laughs, I believe you will find throughout these pages much insight as to what makes life worth living.

Where should you place this book? That also depends on you. It's great on the bedside table for a little read before you turn out the light and go to sleep. It's perfect reading in the bathroom. It's a welcome addition to your bookshelf where you can refer to it every once in a while. Your overnight guests may enjoy delving into it when they find it on the bedside table in the guestroom. Or you can wrap it up and put it under the Christmas tree for someone you feel will enjoy it. Wherever you put it, my aim is to bring much pleasure to you and those you love. For me, it doesn't get any better than that.

From my heart to yours,
Susan Jeffers

1.

The "Pink in the Rug" Syndrome

I STOOD AT THE WINDOW with a smile on my face. My neighbor, who lives below my cliff-side home, had just had his very large tree trimmed—the critical tree that, if not trimmed yearly, would obstruct the magical view of the ocean from my bedroom window. In the back of my mind always lived the disquieting thought that one day he would decide to let the tree grow very, very tall, so I breathed a sigh of relief knowing I wouldn't have to worry about my view until next year—when the height of the tree would once again begin to trouble me.

And then I noticed IT. Just as I was walking away from the window, my eyes focused on THE BRANCH . . . the one branch that should have been removed to make the view absolutely perfect . . . at least to my eyes. Alas, it was too late. The tree trimmers had all gone home and I would have to live with THE BRANCH for an entire year which, for me, was easier said than done.

Unfortunately, every time I looked out of the window at my magical view, all I could see was THE BRANCH! Forget the ocean, the beach, the mountains, the ever-changing sky . . . all I could see was THE BRANCH! No matter how hard I tried NOT to see THE BRANCH, the bigger it seemed to loom.

I was relating this story to my friend, Donna. I said, "Could you believe that I could be that unappreciative of all the beauty out there and focus only on THE BRANCH . . . the one little detail that isn't exactly the way I wanted it?"

"Yes," she said, "I could believe it. I have the same situation with THE PINK IN MY RUG," Donna explained.

It turns out that the long-awaited custom-made carpet for her living room floor had recently been delivered. She had ordered a purple background, a color she had carefully picked to coordinate with other features in the room. After many months, the rug finally arrived and she was distressed to discover that the purple background wasn't purple at all . . . it was PINK. Oh, yes, it went with everything in the room, but it wasn't exactly as she wanted it. She could have had the rug re-made, but that would have cost her a lot of extra money (the rug maker wasn't very cooperative!), and her floor would have remained bare for a few more months. In the end, she decided to keep the rug.

You know where I am going with this. Now, every time she looks in her living room, which is filled with many beautiful things, all she can see is THE PINK IN THE RUG. No matter how hard she tries to blind her eyes to the PINK and focus on everything else that is perfect, the PINK looms before her.

As she related the story, we began to laugh at the ridiculousness of our inability to enjoy all the good as we focused on the one little thing which wasn't exactly as we wanted it. And we called it THE PINK IN THE RUG syndrome.

I know it sounds as though we are just two spoiled brats behaving badly . . . and I'm certain there is some truth to that! But I'm pretty sure that all of us—young or old, rich or poor—can relate to this syndrome. For example . . .

> You had a very successful job interview and you obsess about the one question you wish you had answered differently.

> You score 97 out of 100 points on your final exam . . . and you focus on the three points you didn't get.

> You are having a lovely meal out with family and friends . . . and you focus on the fact that the waiter is too slow.

> Your wedding was magical, but you focus on the fact that the florist forgot to put the yellow freesias in your bouquet.

These are all examples of THE PINK IN THE RUG syndrome. I'm sure you can think of some similar examples in your own life. And you will notice something interesting: the syndrome often involves something that bothers only you and would be totally unnoticed by anyone else. For example . . .

> I never hear anyone looking at my view and saying, "Boy that branch really spoils the view." No, they are in awe of the beauty of it all.

> Donna never hears anyone looking at her living room and asking why she didn't get a purple carpet. No, they comment on the beauty of the room.

People hearing you had a score of 97 wouldn't say, "Why didn't you have a perfect score?" No, they would say, "Well done!"

Most people hearing of your dinner with family and friends wouldn't say, "That's too bad. It's horrible that the waiter was slow." No, they would say, "Lucky you! Having a great dinner with people you love."

And I'm sure that people attending your wedding wouldn't have said, "Not having yellow freesias in your bouquet really messed up your wedding." No, they would have been totally focused on the love in the room.

You get the picture.

So why are most of us afflicted by THE PINK IN THE RUG syndrome? Why can't we focus only on the beauty? I guess it has something to do with the fact that most of us have an intense need to control everything in our lives. And when we don't have that control, we lose our ability to focus on and appreciate all the wonder that actually exists. An eye-opening thought . . .

Maybe we are all spoiled brats, after all!

Certainly children scream and cry when one little thing isn't right in their life. Well, aren't we all screaming and crying in our own way when we focus on one little area that isn't exactly as we wish it to be and refuse to see all the beauty in our lives?

In any case, I'm sorry to say that I haven't yet come up with a remedy for this child-like mentality. But what has helped me greatly is to laugh at this silly syndrome that so clearly symbolizes my need to control everything around me. Whenever I am upset by something in my life, more and more I am able to recognize it as just another example of THE PINK IN THE RUG syndrome . . . and I begin to laugh.

I have discovered that laughter is one of the best medicines for many things, including THE PINK IN THE RUG syndrome. When we can lighten up and laugh, particularly at ourselves, the beauty in our life is appreciated once again. And when we can laugh with a wonderful friend like Donna, the beauty is enhanced 100-fold.

So begin laughing with your best friend, even in the midst of your complaints, and one day you will find yourself—as I did—actually enjoying those PINK IN THE RUG moments that occur occasionally in your own life. In fact, laughing with a friend almost makes the PINK IN THE RUG syndrome a blessing. Think about it.

© 2000 Susan Jeffers, Ph.D.

2.

Saying "YES!" to Breast Cancer

YES! IS MORE THAN A WORD. It is a state of mind that says, "No matter what happens in my life, I'll make something wonderful out of it." I know this sounds difficult when one thinks about the possible losses and disappointments that life sometimes brings, but saying YES! is the antidote to the fear that more often than not accompanies these losses and disappointments. I speak from experience.

Many years ago I had a mastectomy and experienced first hand the many fears involved in having breast cancer. But my choice (and it is a choice!) to say YES! to breast cancer instead of NO!, turned this potentially devastating experience into an enriching one. I talk about my positive experience of breast cancer in all my books and talks hoping it will bring comfort, not only to others in the same situation, but also to those who live in fear of this very prevalent disease. Because of this, I received an award from the Associates of Breast Cancer Studies, a wonderful organization that raises money for the John Wayne Cancer Institute in Santa Monica, California.

I'd like to share with you part of my acceptance speech. It demonstrates how the attitude of YES! can exist even with something as potentially devastating as breast cancer. It demonstrates that the beauty is always there *if you look for it*. That's the key. If you don't look for it, you remain stuck in a victim mentality. . . a very powerless and frightening place to be stuck. And you miss out on so many of the opportunities that even a disease such as cancer can bring. Also in this speech, you will notice the humor. We take things much too seriously in our present day world. Laughter can bring a lot of joy where only upset once prevailed. With these thoughts in mind, here is my acceptance speech:

Tonight I am being honored with the Spirit of Discovery award. This is such an apropos award for me because, impossible as it may seem, breast cancer has indeed offered me a great opportunity for discovery. In fact, I can go so far as to say that breast cancer has been one of the most enriching experiences of my life. Now don't look at me like I'm crazy. Let me explain.

For many years before my illness, I was teaching my students how to say YES! to life . . . how to say YES! to whatever life hands them and to find the beauty no matter how difficult a situation may be. I had learned this philosophy of life after reading and re-reading *Man's Search for Meaning* by Viktor Frankl,[1] a book which, as many of you know, describes his experiences in a concentration camp. He had seen and experienced the worst life had to offer and yet, he learned that there was one thing no one could ever take away from him . . . and that was his reaction to whatever life handed him. And his choice was to react to his horrible

7

experiences in a way that brought much enrichment to his life and to the world.

After the first reading of this inspiring book, I said to myself, "If he can say YES! to something as horrible as a concentration camp, which included the worst kind of treatment one can imagine in addition to the loss of his loved ones, then I can say YES! to anything." And I've tried to live my life with a great big YES! in my heart ever since.

So there I was lying in my hospital bed those many years ago and saying to myself, "OK, Susan, you have a choice now. Are you going to see yourself as a victim, or are you going to say YES! and find the blessing in something as frightening as breast cancer." I thankfully chose the latter. Trust me when I tell you *I didn't understand immediately what possible blessings there could be in breast cancer*, but when I set my sights on looking for the blessings instead of the negatives, I found so many. . . and I am still counting. Let me share some of these blessings with you.

I was dating my present husband, Mark, at the time. I wasn't quite sure where I wanted this relationship to go. I was the "no-need" woman, incredibly independent. He was the workaholic, work coming before everything. When I was diagnosed with breast cancer, he was able to see my vulnerability and dropped everything to be with me. I was able to see the incredible nurturer that emerged from deep within his Soul . . . and I let myself take in all the gifts of love and caring he was giving. This experience was so meaningful to both of us that we decided we wanted to spend the rest of our lives together. So Mark and I got married . . . and so many years later it remains a marriage made in Heaven.

What else did I learn? This is for you women out there. I learned that sexuality had nothing to do with a breast. I have never had a breast re-construction after my mastectomy simply because I did not want to inflict any more trauma on my body. And when I look in the mirror, I do not feel mutilated as some magazine articles suggest I should be feeling. Rather I look at that scar and breathe a sigh of relief and gratitude knowing I've conquered a disease. I celebrate the fact that I am now healthy. And I feel just as sexual as I did before the mastectomy. I learned that sexuality is an attitude, a way of being. It has nothing to do with a breast. In fact, Mark says I look like a sexy pirate!

Another blessing. When Mark used to travel a lot on business, as a joke, I would often put one of my spare prosthesis in his suitcase with a love note. He often bragged that he was the only man he knew who could take his wife's breast with him wherever he goes! Dare I reveal it, but he calls me his "titless wonder!" And I never cease to be thrilled by my title. I feel special.

At the time, I also asked myself if there were any negative emotions I was holding within that could cause disease in my body. More and more, the medical profession is associating negative emotions with disease. As I looked, I couldn't help but notice I was still holding on to a lot of old anger, like many women still hold today. While I liked being angry (it was a very pseudo-powerful feeling!) I decided it was time to let it go . . . to deal with the fear and pain that was lurking behind the anger. I learned that anger could be a cop-out for not taking responsibility for my actions and reactions in life. I stopped casting blame; I took charge of my life; I honored who I was; and I learned how to open my heart. Wow! What a difference an open heart makes in your life! It lets in the sunshine instead of the gloom. My letting go of my anger was also my impetus to writing my second book entitled *Opening Our Hearts to Men.*

Then there was the time I went for a mammogram. As I was paying my bill, the cashier said it was 120 dollars. She looked again and said, "Wait. It's only one side. That's 60 dollars." And I shouted, "YES! I even get to save some money!"

And then there's my teaching. Often when I talk about saying YES! to life, a student will say, "That's easy with the little things. But what about the big things, such as cancer." It's here that I can say, "You sure can say YES! to cancer. I did!" And I am able to tell my story.

And then there's the issue of aging. Someone asked me recently if aging bothered me. I said, "Are you kidding! Once you've had cancer you celebrate every birthday with much greater joy than you ever did before. And so do the many people who love you."

In many ways, cancer is like a wake-up call. It says one never knows how much time one has left in life. So we should stop focusing so much on the future and pay more attention to the simple pleasures of everyday life. And that's what I have learned to do. That first cup of coffee in the morning. YES! The hot shower on the back. YES! The purr of the engine when the key is turned in my car. YES! The beautiful sun warming the very depths of my being. Heaven! I discovered that it's not the grand splashes of brilliance that define a beautiful life. It's the simple pleasures of the NOW. A beautiful lesson indeed. And it was this discovery that eventually led to my book, *End the Struggle and Dance with Life*. You see, it's all grist for the mill!

And then there was the day I received a phone call asking if I would accept the Spirit of Discovery award. Would I accept it!?!

YES!!!

I hope this little acceptance speech conveys in a meaningful way the enormous power in saying YES! to life . . . in looking for the good in any situation we find ourselves . . . even one as potentially devastating as breast cancer. If we focus on the negative, that's what we will get—the negative. If we focus on the positive, that's what we will get—the positive.

I know it's very easy to say YES! when things go right for us. But the trick is saying YES! when things seem to be going badly. We can only do this when we realize there are blessings inherent in all things and our task is to find these blessings. I promise you that this attitude of YES! makes all the difference between a life filled with misery and scarcity or a life filled with joy and abundance. I am forever thankful that I learned I had a choice . . . as we all do.

© 1998 Susan Jeffers, Ph.D.

(To practice saying "YES!" to the Universe, go to *Feel the Fear...and Beyond*)

3.

"Single-Hood": A Journey Into Wholeness

I KNOW THAT MANY OF YOU are single and are dismayed about not being "double." I am here to tell you not to be dismayed. You have a great opportunity for discovering much about becoming whole. I was single for twelve years between my marriages, and I know whereof I speak. I wouldn't have traded that valuable time for anything. I learned first hand that those who lament single-hood are not paying attention to all the value that could be gained and the fun that could be had by being a single person.

One of the problems with those who are unhappy with the singles scene is that they tend to live a very negative kind of life.

"Why didn't he call."
"My life is so boring."
"Everyone's getting married, except me."

I learned from my own experience that if you really want to enjoy those single years, it is time to get rid of the negativity and get "BIGGER" about life.

"I signed up for a great trip!"
"I'm volunteering for a special charity!"
"I'm going back to college!"

It's time to make yours a life of exclamation marks!!! Fill it up with many wonderful things including friends, opportunities for personal growth and contribution to the community.

It is important to avoid the "poor us" conversations with friends. Conversations should be about how much there is to do, to learn and to celebrate about life. And laugh a lot! If your complaint-buddies continue complaining, it's time to change friends. Up-beat friends are so important for keeping spirits high.

It makes sense that if we learn to enjoy single-hood, we will be better equipped to enjoy married-hood. The neediness disappears, the confidence appears, and love is free to radiate out all over the place. Just remember that a great marriage requires two whole people. And single-hood is the perfect arena for learning how to be a whole person. When Mr. Right comes along, it's nice when Ms. Right is there to greet him, and vice versa.

Always remember that neediness is an enemy of love. We are told that one of the greatest love stories ever written is *Romeo and Juliet*. Between you and me, it really is one of the sickest love stories ever written! (Sorry about that, Shakespeare!) Two teenagers who kill themselves because they couldn't live without each other. Pathetic! I suspect the relationship would have broken up in six months anyway. Why? Because they were too needy! Neediness eventually turns into blame. "Why aren't you making me happy?" Goodbye, relationship! Does this sound familiar?

I think we're all tired of such child-like scenarios. We'd much prefer a really grown-up and satisfying kind of love. To me. . .

A healthy love isn't about someone filling us up; it's about filling ourselves up . . . with great company by our side.

Whether we are in a relationship or not, the first step toward attaining a grown-up love is to create a rich, balanced life for ourselves.

Life is HUGE! It is up to each and every one of us to become a part of it all. When we do, our neediness disappears. We are fulfilled. And our ability to love with a sense of confidence and joy radiates throughout our being. We become a magnet to all that is good in this world. . . and that includes a truly wonderful relationship.

Understand that the states of single-hood and married-hood can BOTH bring great rewards. The sweet secret is to enjoy the rewards of whatever state you're in. I know of no better way to guarantee that the grass is always greenest wherever you find yourself standing.

© 2001 Susan Jeffers, Ph.D.

4.

Eyeball to Eyeball:
Why Shorter Men Are Better

NOTE: I wrote this in 1985, the year Mark and I got married, and it still makes me smile.

I'M HERE TO DISPEL THE "TALL" part of the myth of the "tall, dark and handsome man." By now, I consider myself an expert, having spent much of my life looking UP trying to find the man of my dreams. Actually, I found quite a number of likely candidates . . . but there was always a vague kind of discomfort about the whole thing . . . usually in the area of the neck! Oh, to be sure, I was approached by shorter versions of the male species, but I scoffed at their attention. Mother had trained me that TALL was definitely better! Good old Mom . . .

Thankfully, there was one short man who got through to me like no other man ever had. He wouldn't take no for an answer. He persisted until I no longer resisted. The height barrier simply had to go. It was only then that I discovered what I had been missing all those years! Just in case you, too, have been living with the delusion that only tall men are terrific, let me share just a few of the highlights of my new discovery. It may change your life dramatically.

To begin with, taking a walk has become an exhilarating experience. Shoulder to shoulder—we can comfortably chat, enjoying each other's view of the world. Contrast this with days gone by when I constantly found myself tripping over uneven pavements or falling into potholes. It seemed that unless I kept looking up at my date's lips, I had great difficulty understanding what he was saying. I surmised that sound must travel upwards—either that or I was becoming terribly hard of hearing. In either case, the problem has now been solved.

Even standing together on a street corner has taken on new dimensions. It's so nice being able to just reach over to give his cheek an affectionate kiss as we wait for the light to change. And his lips are just THERE for the tasting—no more gymnastics trying to jump up to make my mark (which, much to my embarrassment, I usually missed).

And then there's the matter of stride. My walks with a tall man always seemed to end up as an awkward jog—three of my steps to every one of his. A graceful figure, I was not! While it might have been healthy aerobically speaking, I don't think it did much to enhance good relationships. Old beaus were always yelling at me to hurry up and I was always panting painfully, pleading with them to slow down. Compromise seemed impossible. Now the scene is very different. My sweetheart and I enjoy our walks in perfect unison—hands entwined to ensure an added measure of togetherness. (Now, it's only passion that keeps me panting!)

I mustn't forget to mention my foot doctor's pleasure about my new romance. He's been after me for years to stop wearing high-heeled shoes. My metatarsal arches were rebelling. I explained that high-heeled shoes were a MUST with tall men. When I wore flat shoes, it felt like I was walking on my knees! What's worse, it looked like it too! But I knew, deep down, that my foot doctor was right—my feet were always killing me. My dates thought I was a little strange when, in abject pain, I would ask them if they would mind carrying me home. Usually they refused and were always a bit embarrassed when I took off my shoes and walked barefoot down Park Avenue. One was particularly embarrassed when we were walking with his boss.

But now my foot problems are over. I wouldn't think of wearing high-heeled shoes and upset the delicate balance. As a matter of fact, I've recently given away a closet-full of beautiful high-heeled shoes to very grateful friends. They promised the shoes would be returned to me if the relationship ever broke up. (Shoes are rather expensive these days.) But I've informed them that I have no intention of giving up such a perfect match—and my excuse for wearing flat shoes!

Not only is walking an enhanced experience . . . can you imagine what has happened to dancing? Somehow I never found it very romantic having my face muffled against a suit jacket—or the alternative, straining my neck as I looked upward, struggling for air. But now dancing is heaven as we float around the dance floor—cheek to cheek. As I put both my arms around his neck and he puts both his hands around my waist, dancing becomes a perpetual hug—heartbeat to heartbeat. Other couples look at us enviously and try clumsily to emulate our cozy position—the men hunched down and the women standing on their toes—but they never get it together the way we do.

Which brings us to the matter of making love . . .what can I say! Eyeball to eyeball, lip to lip, belly to belly . . . need I go any further!!! Pure unadulterated satisfaction! And then there's the delicious dessert of sweetly snuggling afterwards—aligned and entwined in each other's arms. Foot to foot—it's a perfect fit!

And would you believe I even discovered a woman's lib benefit to loving a short man? Personally, I've always found it very difficult trying to be an equal with someone who is gorilla sized. Big men (poor things) always brought out the "pouting child" part of me that demanded to be taken care of. I never seemed to want to grow up. I must admit it didn't feel very good. At my age, the "little girl" image was a bit unflattering.

But with my new man, I feel like a WOMAN! While he takes care of me beautifully, I have an intense desire to take care of him as well. His equal size makes him appear softer, more vulnerable—certainly more loveable—than all the rest. He arouses the compassionate and caring me—the part of me I like best. And think about this: If you must look up at him, he must look down at you! Metaphorically speaking, this is a no-no!

I think you now have the total picture—eyeball to eyeball, lip to lip, belly to belly, toe to toe. A match made in heaven. Mom, can I tell you something—heart to heart? You were definitely wrong. Shorter men are better . . . at least my man is . . .

© 1985 Susan Jeffers, Ph.D.

5.

Don't Let Rejection Stop You!

THE JOURNEY TO SUCCESS can sometimes be very discouraging and sometimes we are tempted to pick up all our toys and go home when the going gets a little rough. I certainly experienced that feeling many times in my attempt to become a published writer but I pursued and pursued until I ultimately achieved success.

A little background: For many years, I had tried to sell my very first book which I titled, *Feel the Fear And Do It Anyway*. After many, many rejections from just as many publishers, I woefully put the book proposal into a drawer and went on with my life.

Three years passed. One day I was going through the contents of the very same drawer that housed my sadly rejected and long forgotten first attempt at a writing career. I picked my book proposal up. . . looked at it. . . paged through it. . . and all of a sudden, I was struck with the powerful sense that I held something in my hands that would be of help to many people. And, once again, but this time with a very strong resolve, I set out to find an agent and a publisher who believed in my book the same way I did. And this time, I succeeded. What's more I succeeded beyond my wildest dreams.

I thought it would give you some encouragement if I shared with you parts of the rejection letters that my wonderfully patient agent, Dominick Abel (three other agents had given up on me!) received from publishers to whom he submitted the book proposal for *Feel the Fear And Do It Anyway*. They may give you hope in your quest for success in whatever arena you choose to pursue . . . and a laugh or two. Naturally, I won't name the editors who wrote these comments . . . even the best are sometimes wrong. (That's an important thing to remember.) So, here they are . . . just a few of the many!

"I don't think that Susan Jeffers is ready yet for a book publication. I like her writing, I like her enthusiasm and, of course, I always celebrate change. The supporting material is thin as it stands, and she has not yet attained the visibility to sell her book in the national market. This material may lend itself to an article but certainly not a book. I'm sorry, but it's not for me now."

"Although I see the merit in this idea, I'm just not turned on by her writing."

"There's been a glut of self-help books in the last few years and our figures indicate that the sales in this area are down considerably. To take on a book in this category it would have to be almost revolutionary and I didn't feel that way about this proposal."

"Thanks very much for letting us consider Susan Jeffers' proposal for *Feel the Fear And Do It Anyway*. It's quite nicely done. But my colleagues aren't enthusiastic about the commercial appeal of the subject itself and think we'd have a difficult time selling the book."

"This is an exceptionally strong proposal but it's in a field which we unfortunately feel is glutted. Susan Jeffers is a savvy, articulate writer and this book has a lot of good stuff in it. Her approach may even be utterly original—but the sense here is that it won't work in this glutted market."

"We will not be bidding on this book. We feel that there is too much competition now out there for this book, and it'll be an uphill battle to sell this book."

And the best rejection of them all . . .

"Lady Di could be bicycling nude down the street giving this book away and no one would read it."

You can see why I wanted to pick up my toys and go home. Thankfully, I didn't . . . nor did Dominick! He stuck with me and ultimately we made the first sale to Harcourt Brace Jovanovich. A wonderful editor there, named Martha Lawrence, (who now is the author of delightful mystery novels) saw the value in the book and bought it. The rest is history, as they say: After YEARS of trying, *Feel the Fear And Do It Anyway* was finally published in 1987. It has now sold millions and millions of copies and is presently available in over 100 countries and has been translated into over 35 languages. And these figures are growing every day.

I have received mail from all over the world with thanks for the words that I wrote. It seems that the reading of this book has helped so many people in so many ways. Some credited it with actually saving their lives. Wow! Thank goodness for that precious moment in time when I had the inner "knowing" that this book would make a difference in people's lives.

So in the world according to Susan Jeffers, when you have a dream, don't give up. While you may be rejected, those who are doing the rejecting may not know what a treasure they are holding in the palm of their hand. As long as YOU know in the depth of your heart that you have something wonderful to offer this world, in whatever form that is, you will have persistence . . . and a much greater chance of making your dreams come true.

So FEEL THE FEAR AND DO IT ANYWAY . . . and if it doesn't work one way, try another . . . and another . . . and another. Keep exploring. See where your efforts lead you. Be open to new experiences. The possibilities are limitless!

6.

A "Child" Grows Up on Valentine's Day

I WANT TO TELL YOU a very beautiful Valentine's story. A friend of mine, Karen, was asked by her teenage son, Jeff, if she could think of anything special he could do with his girlfriend on Valentine's Day . . . in addition to the traditional romantic dinner. He truly wanted to make a good impression.

Karen thought for a moment and said, "Why don't you go down to the supermarket and buy 50 roses . . . they are very inexpensive right now and I'll help you pay for them. The roses are not for your girlfriend, however. I suggest that both of you visit a home for the elderly and give everyone there one of the roses. That would be a very loving thing to do. And I believe your girlfriend would be very pleased." He wasn't expecting this kind of a suggestion but, much to his credit, he decided to do it.

Karen then called one of the local homes for the elderly and asked if it would be all right for Jeff to come by with his girlfriend and pass around the roses. The nurse who picked up the phone was more than enthusiastic; she was ecstatic! "No one has ever done anything like this before," she said, "and it would make such a difference to the people here."

Jeff and his girlfriend showed up at the appointed hour a little nervous, not knowing what to expect. But they soon got into the swing of things as they went around the home for the elderly passing out the roses, smiling, talking and giving everyone there the feeling that somebody cared. He came back home thrilled that his date went well . . . but much more thrilled at a significant discovery, and that was . . . his life makes a difference. He was able to make people feel good with his simple acts of caring. When Karen told me this story, I was so moved that I cried! I also noted that Jeff's girlfriend must have fallen in love with him for life!

I believe that my friend, Karen, has come up with the cure for some of the ills we see in so many of our children in today's world. So few young people are called upon to help those around them. Our society focuses on the importance of winning—which is very alienating; it doesn't focus on the importance of giving—which is very joyful. As a result, we are left with an abundance of self-absorbed "brats" who truly don't realize that their lives make a difference. Perhaps the greatest thing we can teach our children is that they DO make a difference. The only way they can learn this important fact is to expose them to ways they can give to the world around them.

As Karen told me her story, I remembered back to a story one of my workshop attendees told me. It was Christmas and after opening a multitude of presents, all her six-year-old daughter had to say was, "Is that all?" Exasperated, she came up with a plan that turned everything around. Starting the following January, she and her daughter started making little gifts for the purpose of distributing them to patients in a local hospital the following Christmas. As the months passed, her daughter got more and more excited about the approaching Christmas . . . not because of what she was going to GET but because of what she was going to GIVE. Powerful.

My children were lucky. For the ten years I was Executive Director of The Floating Hospital in New York City, they were exposed to the joy in giving as they volunteered to help whenever they could. To this day, they are involved with various projects to help the poor and to save the environment. I applaud them for caring so much. My daughter said that whenever she feels bad about anything in her life, the solution is easy: She gets herself out of the house and finds a way to help others. It works all the time by making her realize how important her life is to others in this world. Beautiful!

The implication of all I have told you is so simple. It is so obvious. Yet it is overlooked:

The way we build self-esteem in our children is to teach them to act in ways that build self-esteem.

Telling children repeatedly how wonderful they are doesn't make them feel wonderful about themselves. Showing them how to act in ways that help the world around them DOES make them feel wonderful about themselves. Come to think of it, perhaps this is a good lesson for all of us adults as well!

© 2000 Susan Jeffers, Ph.D.

7.

The News: Fact or Fiction

I was rather naïve in earlier days. I truly believed that the producers of television news had our best interests at heart, wanting us to see all sides of the picture so that we could make educated decisions in our own lives. I know that some of these ethical producers do exist (I've met some) but I had an interesting experience that made me healthily skeptical as to what I hear on television. Let me tell you about it so that you, too, will watch the news with an alert and much more questioning eye.

I RECEIVED A PHONE CALL from a Public Relations (PR) agent who asked me if I wanted to appear on a national news show the following day to discuss the results of a study that had just been released. This particular study compared children who were being cared for exclusively by their mothers with children who were in day care. The stated results of this study were that the more hours a young child spends in day care or with various care-takers, the more aggressive they are when they enter kindergarten. This was considered very bad news for working mothers, indeed!

I told her I would love to do the show as I knew a lot about the problems of research in the field of human behavior and could shed some light on the subject . . . and, of course, a national show would offer me a wonderful opportunity to promote my new book, *I'm Okay . . . You're a Brat.*

A few minutes later I got a call from one of the show's producers. She told me it would be a short segment and that I would be up "against" another expert. One of us would be there to put the blame on parents for putting their children in day-care and one of us would be there to put the blame on the care-takers for the bad practices that created these "frightening" results. She then asked which side I wanted to take.

Knowing what I know about research (a field I have studied with great interest), I calmly explained to the producer that:

> One study doesn't prove anything. What it does offer is a spring-board for further investigation.

> The design of the study and/or interpretation of the results could be seriously flawed, and, as a result, she could be sending the wrong message to the listening audience.

> There most likely was another study out there that showed the opposite results!

For these and other reasons, I said that presenting such an argument is hurtful to everyone concerned—parents, care-takers and children alike—particularly to those women who had no choice but to send their children to day-care. And she would be doing so on potentially false premises. I suggested that it would be much better if I could be there to explain to parents what to watch for in research projects so they could make up their own minds.

I didn't realize I was talking to a wall! As if she didn't hear a word I said, she asked, "So, which side do you want to take . . . the one against the parents or the one against day-care facilities?" Aagh!

At this point, I had to tell her that I couldn't do the show. Needless to say, she was a bit surprised. Trust me when I tell you that most of us who are considered experts in any field very much want to get on national television to share our ideas . . . and, of course, to promote our books. But at some point, one has to draw a line. I drew the line. And she went off to find another expert who would go along with the premise of the show . . . which of course she found.

As could be predicted, all the 24 hour cable channels plus the national media picked up the story of this child-care study and the "debate" went on for days and days with mothers bearing the brunt of the attacks. I watched in dismay. Who knows how many mothers quit their jobs and went home . . . out of guilt, not out of choice . . . when in many cases they and their children would have been far better served by the stimulation of a job and an enriching day-care environment?

One week later, after all the massive coverage stirred up by the intense media coverage, I wasn't surprised to see it reported in the Los Angeles Times that *the child-care study in question was seriously flawed for a number of reasons including the erroneous interpretation of the data. Therefore, no conclusions can be drawn from it.* I investigated further and discovered that . . .

Even though the children were a bit more aggressive, *the children's aggressive behavior was in the normal range.*

"Hostility" as described by the researchers seemed to be a healthy—not an unhealthy—sign.

There was no follow-up in terms of how the children's "hostility" level was a few months later. Perhaps it all evened out in a very short time.

Two researchers involved in the research project said the media was extrapolating too much from the conclusions, particularly since the lead researcher was very biased in his interpretation.

In many areas (for example, language and memory skills) *children from day care centers actually performed BETTER than children raised solely by their mothers.*

And, of course, these differences in the two groups could be explained by an unknown third factor that wasn't even considered in the study.

Now for the REALLY, REALLY bad news: I listened carefully but . . .

I NEVER HEARD ONE CORRECTION OR APOLOGY OR RETRACTION FROM THOSE PROGRAMS THAT CREATED THE MISINFORMATION AND CONTROVERSY TO BEGIN WITH!

In fact, long after the results of the study were shown to be erroneous, one news commentator, with a great display of ignorance, actually used the study as proof that parents should be wary of putting their children in day-care. Ouch!

What can we learn from the above? It is important that we question what we hear in the news. Yes, there are many producers and experts with a high degree of integrity and intelligence. But this isn't always so. Also, more and more, we are learning that sensationalism rules and very often the material presented by desperate producers and "pseudo-experts" isn't truthful or accurate. When you have 24-hour news broadcasts, the competition for ratings is fierce and the material is scarce. Therefore, news is often invented, slanted, inflated and/or manipulated, as was being done here.

The above is only one example of the many distortions that are being fed to us by some members of the media under the guise of fact . . . whether it has to do with health, politics, child-rearing, the state of the world, or whatever. We would be wise to listen with a sense of healthy skepticism. Maybe they're right; maybe they're wrong. If the subject matter interests or affects us, we need to investigate on our own. And often, it is our own gut feeling that ultimately leads us to the truth.

8.

Why Do People Scoff at the Idea of "Self-Help"?

THERE ARE MANY PEOPLE who turn their noses up at the idea of "Self-Help". I have never understood why. Perhaps they just don't understand. After all, isn't it common-sense for us to gather the tools to help ourselves live a wonderful life? And to me that's what Self-Help is all about. Certainly the Self-Help Movement was a blessing to me and is now the basis of all my writings. Let me tell you my story.

As I explain in my very first book, *Feel the Fear And Do It Anyway*, I used to be an incredibly fearful person. Because of my intense fear, it is not surprising that I hung onto many things that clearly were not working for me. I longed to move forward with my life but fear was holding me back. Part of my problem was the non-stop little voice inside my head that kept telling me very negative things such as, "You'd better not change your situation." "Don't take a chance." "You might make a mistake." "You're not good enough." And on and on and on.

My fear never seemed to abate. Even my doctorate in psychology didn't seem to do me much good! Then one day, as I was dressing for work, I reached the turning point. As I glanced in the mirror, I saw an all-too-familiar sight—eyes red and puffy from tears of self-pity. Suddenly a good healthy rage welled up inside me, and I began shouting at my reflection in the mirror, "ENOUGH . . . ENOUGH . . . ENOUGH!" I shouted and shouted and shouted until there were no shouts left.

When I stopped, I felt a strange and wonderful sense of relief and calm that I had never felt before. Without realizing it at the time, I had gotten in touch with a very powerful part of myself that before that moment I hadn't even known existed. I took another long look in the mirror and smiled as I nodded my head YES. The old familiar voice of doom and gloom was drowned out, at least temporarily, and a new voice had come to the fore— one that felt healthy and strong. My rage had been transformed into a feeling of strength, love, joy . . . and all good things.

At that moment I knew I was never again going to let fear get the better of me. I would find a way to rid myself of the negativity that prevailed in my life. Thus began my Spiritual odyssey, the Journey to the best of who I am.

Over the years, with the help of a WIDE variety of teachers, I gathered many tools and I learned many things: I learned that what I thought was the totality of my being was only an infinitesimally small part of a much larger whole; I learned that there were dimensions of my being that I had never experienced or explored; I learned that as much as I got caught in the melodrama of daily life, there was a more transcendent way of seeing myself in this world; I learned that I had an immense amount of power and love living inside me.

It is this Spiritual odyssey, the Journey to the best of who we are, which I believe is at the heart of the Self-Help Movement.

This Spiritual odyssey is about finding the fantastic power and love we hold inside . . . and then radiating that power and love out into the world. It is a Journey to that something wondrous within our being . . . our Higher Self. And it is more . . .

- It is about learning how to focus on our blessings. We are masters for taking things for granted . . . and taking things for granted is one of the greatest assaults on our lives. We must learn to notice the wonder of it all . . . the blessings all around us. We must practice gratitude. We have to learn how to make all the ordinary events in our lives extraordinary . . . because that is what they are.
- It is also about trust . . . trusting there is a reason, a purpose for all that happens in our lives and the lives of those we love. And using all of our experiences to learn and to grow.
- It is about learning how to let go of the victim mentality and taking responsibility for our experience of life. "Victims" live in the Lower Self. "Creators" live in the Higher Self.
- It is about living in the now. Our goals are wonderful, but they are not our life. NOW is our life! The joy of the process is more important than the actual reaching of our goals.
- It is about making this a better world. It is about healing a very sick planet. It is about "being" love and teaching love.

As you read the above, you realize that the Self-Help Movement is nothing to scoff at! In fact, why would anyone resist!

Of course, you will sometimes find teachers in the Self-Help Movement who ought not to be teaching. (I certainly found some in this category!) For some reason, they are not equipped to help people become the best that they can be. Also, some teachers are perfect for some, but not for others. So much depends upon who we are and what we need at any given moment of time.

But, not to worry! In the end, the essence of the Self-Help Movement as I see it is about learning to trust yourself. If something feels right for you, give it a try. If it doesn't, let it go. Little by little, as you practice "trusting your gut", you will be led to many wonderful places. It is a vast field filled with many avenues to travel. That's what makes it so exciting. The Self-Help Journey is an amazing Journey, indeed!

9.

Some Enchanted Evening

**You gaze across that proverbial crowded room . . .
and there he (or she) is. You've finally found the
love of your life.**

OH, IF ONLY IT WERE SO! Yes, it happens sometimes
. . . but rarely. Generally speaking finding someone to love
isn't that easy. Indeed, there seem to be many roadblocks
to finding a successful relationship. And while we may
blame circumstances "out there" for our inability to
romantically connect, we would do better to "pick up the
mirror instead of the magnifying glass" (I can hear the
groans from here!) and look at some of the beliefs we hold
inside. Understand that this is not to blame ourselves, but
to empower ourselves.

I introduced this valuable tool in *Opening Our Hearts
to Men* and have used it often in subsequent books. You
will find it mentioned in a number of articles throughout
this book as well. It is a very important tool for making
positive changes in all areas of your life. After many years
of picking up the mirror myself, here are a few of the
many things I have learned about finding love . . .

It Isn't About Looks! As an experiment, the next time you walk down the street or go to a party, pay attention to the amazing array of couple-combinations that are right before your eyes. Tall, short, thin, fat, beautiful, not so beautiful, and so on. We see that looks play a very small part in our ability to create a loving relationship. We must stop worrying about externals and start paying attention to the size of their hearts . . . and ours!

Be the Kind of Person You Would Like to Date. Many negative and angry men and women put in their order for a positive and emotionally healthy mate. Little do they know that their order is unlikely to be filled . . . an emotionally healthy person would be running the other way! What you put out is usually what you attract. (You can see why that mirror is so important!) It's really that simple. Hence, it stands to reason that we should all make a list of those characteristics that we would like to see in a potential mate and then . . . go about cultivating them in ourselves! Ouch! This may hurt, but I have to admit that my whole life changed when I acted upon this amazing truth.

Your Type Is Not Your Type. If you are not in a successful relationship, one can only surmise that you are attracted to people who are not right for you. I figured this out after many, many relationships between my marriages. I had a good time dating, mind you, but I didn't find someone to love. And one day, there he was. The problem was . . . I was not attracted to him! He wasn't my type.

Thankfully, he pursued. And one day I picked up the mirror and asked myself, "Why are you NOT attracted to someone who is loving, giving and all good things?" My mirror told me that it was my "habit" to be attracted to a specific type who did not suit me at all and, if I wanted to find a beautiful love, I would have to break my habit and change my type! That is what I did . . . and our marriage of many years proves that my mirror was right.

The lesson? We need to re-train ourselves to be attracted to those qualities in a potential mate that support the best of who we are. These, of course, include love, respect, caring, encouragement and all the other qualities that make a long-term relationship a joyous experience.

It's Perfectly Okay for Women to Make the First Approach. With few exceptions, I learned that most men LOVE to have women approach them. When I interviewed a number of men, they presented some very poignant statements about how difficult it is to constantly have to make the first approach as they are often rejected. While women often use the excuse that men don't like it when women make the first approach, let me suggest that what underlies women's resistance to approaching men is that they are frightened of putting themselves in the position of being rejected. Sound familiar? Once women realize that it is only their fear that stops them from approaching men, they can begin to "feel the fear and do it anyway!"

Rejection Isn't to be Taken Personally. When we approach someone, we have to keep reminding ourselves, "No matter how this person acts toward me, I know I am a worthwhile person." While we cannot control someone else's actions, we can definitely control our reactions. Also it is important to remember that, if someone is not interested in getting to know us, there is always someone else who is looking for love.

Don't Trust Body Language. Many men and women report that they turn away from those they are MOST interested in knowing simply because they feel so insecure! So what's the solution? The answer is to go after what YOU want, despite what someone's body language is telling you. You may be pleasantly surprised to find someone to love.

Stop Trying to Be a Mind Reader. "What do women want?!?" "What do men want!?!" These frequently asked questions always get an unexpected answer from me: "It doesn't matter what they want. Be yourself and see who shows up!" I can guarantee you that, if you honor the essence of who you really are and proudly let it shine through, your chances for a successful "match" are greatly increased.

Do What You Love to Do . . . And the Dates Will Follow. Where is the best place to meet people? It's not at home waiting for Prince or Princess Charming to show up. The best place to meet people is wherever people congregate to do the things you love to do. My suggestion is to do NOTHING in your life simply for the purpose of meeting someone. Do something simply because you love to do it . . . because it expands the richness of your life . . . because it brings you pleasure. It is very likely that a person to love will appear when and where you very least expect it.

Develop a Kindness Toward Members of the Opposite Sex. There is much evidence that the war between the sexes has not ended. I guarantee that unless you truly think about and treat members of the opposite sex with kindness and respect you're not going to develop a healthy romantic relationship with any one of them. Many men and women are truly angry at members of the opposite sex, some more openly than others. Each claims good cause for anger. Yes, women, it's true some men will walk all over you. And, yes, men, it's true some women will walk all over you as well. But, in the end, we have to pick up the mirror and discover . . .

We can't blame anyone for walking all over us. We can only notice that we're not getting out of the way.

It is amazing what happens when we stand tall, take charge of our lives and act with integrity toward ourselves and others. Our lives begin to work and we begin to attract people with the same kind of positive energy. And contrary to popular opinion, there are plenty of people with positive energy around. But to find them, it is essential that we pick up the mirror and work through our own anger, lack of trust, judgment, self-righteousness and neediness, all of which are huge barriers to loving one another.

It is a given that the more power and love we radiate to members of the opposite sex, the more powerful and loving are the people we will attract. (Of course, the opposite is true as well!) I believe that it is only when we finally learn to open our hearts to each other that we will find wonderful people to love. That's just the way it is.

You'll have to admit, by picking up the mirror, I certainly learned a lot! You will too.

© 2000 Susan Jeffers, Ph.D.
Adapted from *Dare to Connect*

(You can learn much more about connection in all areas of your life in *Dare to Connect.*)

10.

If You Were Really Important . . .

IT WAS A SIMPLE ASSIGNMENT . . . just off the top of my head. I didn't realize how powerful it was.

In one of my workshops, I instructed all my students to "expand the bottom line" by participating full out in their jobs for one entire week. Novel idea! They were to "act-as-if" their actions really made a difference to everyone around them. The key question they were to constantly ask themselves throughout each day was . . .

"If I were really important here, what would I be doing?"

And then they were to set about "doing it."

Peggy sitting in the third row resisted the assignment. She lamented that she hated her job and was just biding her time until she found a new one. Each day was pure drudgery as she watched the clock slowly move through the eight painful hours. With great skepticism, she finally agreed to try it for just one week . . . to expand her bottom line by committing 100 percent to her job knowing that she really counted.

The following week, as I watched Peggy walk into the room, I couldn't believe the difference in her energy level. When I asked her what was going on, she excitedly reported the events of her week:

"My first step was to brighten up the dismal office with some plants and posters. I then started to really pay attention to the people I work with. If someone seemed unhappy, I asked if there was anything wrong and if I could help. If I went out for coffee, I always asked if there was anything I could bring back for the others. I complimented people. I invited two people for lunch. I told the boss something wonderful about one of my co-workers. (Usually I'm selling myself!)

Then I asked myself how I could improve things for the company itself. First I stopped complaining about the job—I realized I was such a nag! I became a self-starter and came up with a few very good ideas which I began implementing. Every day I made a list of things I wanted to accomplish and I set about accomplishing them. I was really surprised by how much I could do in a day when I focused on what I was doing! I also noticed how fast the day goes by when I am involved.

I put a sign on my desk that said,

"If I were really important here, what would I be doing?"

And every time I started to fall back into my old patterns of boredom and complaining, the sign reminded me of what I was supposed to be doing. That really helped.

It is amazing to me that by just asking myself this question I was able to create such a great work experience for myself . . . and for everybody else!"

What a difference a simple expansion of the bottom line made in just one short week! It made Peggy feel connected to everyone and everything around her—including the organization itself. And it made her enjoy her job for the first time since she had been hired.

While she knew it would soon be time to move on to another job, she realized that while she was still there it was in everyone's best interest, particularly her own, to create an environment of commitment and caring. After all, who wants to spend their days in an energy filled with alienation, boredom and negativity? (I would find it strange if anyone answered YES to that question!) It is also worth noting that with such positive energy, the likelihood of Peggy getting a great recommendation and finding a new, more challenging job would be greatly increased.

I hope Peggy's story has convinced each and every one of you to "act-as-if you were really important" in all aspects of your own lives. Trust me when I tell you that there will come a day when you discover you don't have to "act-as-if" any more. Why? Because you finally realize YOU TRULY ARE IMPORTANT! No acting required!

© 1992 Susan Jeffers, Ph.D.

(For many more "expand the bottom line" tools, go to *Dare To Connect*.)

11.

A New Look at Wrinkles

IT WAS ONE OF THOSE SWEET mellow evenings a number of years ago as my daughter and I sat around talking about what we wanted to be "when we grew up." "How strange," I remarked to her, "that a mother and daughter can sit around talking about what we both wanted to be when we grew up. I wonder if I will ever 'settle down.'" Her answer surprised me. "I certainly hope not! It's your attitude about life that keeps you so young!" Naturally I didn't believe a word of it. Surely the secret of my youthfulness was to be found in the vats of cosmetics on which I spent a fortune annually. They promised eternal youth and I believed them!

I forgot about our conversation until a few weeks later when I was having dinner with a favorite friend who was visiting me from Tucson, Arizona. I sat contemplating her wonderfully vibrant face, energy emanating from every pore, and her blue eyes sparkling as she described her plans for the next few months. I asked myself how she could appear so youthful—after all, she was 65 years old and her face was heavily lined from years of working with the Indians in the Arizona desert.

My conversation with my daughter came back to me. My friend hasn't decided what she wants to be when she grows up either! She is always in the middle of some wonderful adventure. And it definitely is this attitude about life that gives her a quality of agelessness. My daughter was right! I began to relax. Maybe I don't have to worry so much about my wrinkles! Knowing my friend, I'm sure she'd faint if she ever found out what I spend on cosmetics each year! No, her secret of youth is not to be found in a bottle, but in the fact that she will never "settle down."

Perhaps I should explain in case you are getting the wrong impression. Not wanting to "settle down" in the way I am using it does not imply the abdication of responsibility or commitment. In fact, some of the most "non-settled" people I know are those who are passionate, enthusiastic and deeply committed to their pursuits. The key is that they continue to see what they are doing at any given time as only one chapter in a much longer book. They never know how it's going to end, but they are sure that a lot of exciting things will happen before they reach the last chapter. My Arizona friend offers a perfect example.

Her second husband died last year after only five years of a wonderful marriage. She cared for him the last two years of his life as cancer permeated his body. When he died, she deeply mourned his death, as it had taken her many years to find such a special relationship. Then, after a few months, she decided to have a party to celebrate his life. Friends and family came to celebrate with her. It was a tribute to a beautiful man, and it was a tribute to her as well. She never saw the tragedy in his death. She simply felt the privilege of the five years she had with him.

After a brief and healthy period of mourning, the question she asked herself was, "What's next?" She really sees the world as a feast and her only problem is deciding which morsel to taste first. By the way, what a turn-on to men! They pursue her all the time. Her depth, coupled with a sense of reaching out, acts as a magnet. She has an incredible electricity and sexuality about her. Yet, she certainly does not have the outer "attractiveness" that we see in our magazines. It all comes from inside.

I smile as I think of the last time I saw her. I was living in London at the time and she had come to visit on her way to Edinburgh. It was a stormy morning in December as she waved goodbye to me from the train that was taking her to her destination. What lured her to Edinburgh was an ad in her local newspaper reporting that castles were cheap in Scotland. It occurred to her that a castle would be a wonderful place in which to start a center for the prevention of disease, something she had been thinking about for a long time. While she had relatively little money, she felt she could find a way to get enough people interested to raise the money. So there she was on her way to Scotland to search for a castle!

Yes, my friend at 65 is one of the most youthful people I know—or maybe youthful is the wrong word. I think we need an additional age category called TIMELESS. If you think about it, so many qualities are erroneously labeled youthful when they don't really apply to youth at all— qualities such as vibrancy, curiosity, sexiness, liveliness and a sense of adventure. They simply are personality characteristics you can have at any age. I know sexy people at 15 and I know sexy people over 65. I know vibrant people at

15 and I know vibrant people at 65. And so on. So much of it is about lifestyle and outlook, not about age. Perhaps if we learn to refer to those qualities as TIMELESS rather than youthful, we can start to pull away from some of the stigma and fear about aging. We can say "she has a time-less quality" rather than "she has a youthful quality."

The allegories about aging need to be changed as well. What is more depressing than the idea of life going from spring to summer to autumn to winter. What could be bleaker than contemplating "the winter of our lives"! That is, of course, unless you're talking about spending a few romantic months skiing in Switzerland with the man or woman in your life!

Garson Kanin wrote an inspiring book entitled *It Takes a Long Time to Become Young.*[1] I agree. Many young people are so bogged down with the heaviness of inexperience. Everything is a crisis. So much is serious and black. Aging, thankfully, can bring with it an openness, a lightness, a blooming and a richness of spirit. Certainly the older I get, the more spring-like I feel . . . and it shows in the men that are attracted to me. The older I get, the younger they get!

It was not long ago that the thought of dating a younger man turned me off. One of my ways of remaining young was to date much older men. With them I always felt like "the kid". I then met a man seven years my junior who wouldn't take no for an answer. He kept pursuing and luckily for the both of us, I succumbed to his affections. Eventually we decided to live together (and we ultimately married.)* In the beginning, it was not easy.

*My "younger man" and I have been married for 19 years. Heaven!

Unfortunately, he has one of those perennially youthful faces. I compared every wrinkle on my face to the non-existent wrinkles on his face.

I'm happy to report that it did not take me long to get over my panic about the difference in our ages. He finally convinced me that what excites him about me is my appreciation of my own sexuality and my interesting way of seeing the world—both of which have come from the richness of my experiences over the years. Little by little, my initial hesitancy has evaporated. I no longer have any desire to play the role of "the kid."

But just so cosmetic manufacturers don't slit their wrists thinking about the decline in business as a result of my new way of thinking, let me assure them that their bottles still line my bathroom shelves. I'm much more secure, ever since I had my revelations about timelessness, but not THAT secure. It will take me a long time to totally appreciate that women are delicious at any age. Conditioning dies hard, I'm afraid . . . but I think I've made a good start.

© 1984 Susan Jeffers, Ph.D.

12.

Bring Back the Field of Honor!

OVER THE YEARS, we have watched competition in all areas of life sink lower and lower into an unhealthy state of "win at any cost". This is particularly evident in the arena of sports. Certainly, our focus on "winning" as the only goal has soured the entire athletic arena to a deadly degree.

We need only notice how the malevolence of competition has traveled all the way from our children's schoolyards to the once noble Olympic events. Terrible injuries, violence, anger, upset, self-flagellation and even death, are all part of the scene. Yet, I have heard so many claim that the athletic field is "a training ground for cooperation." While there may be pockets of playing fields where this is true, generally speaking, it is not true. In fact, the title of a 1994 CNN television show about sports, *Field of Screams*, is very revealing.

For a while, I abhorred the concept of competition so much that, if there was a vote, I would have made it illegal. A bit difficult in a world where competition is considered to be the backbone of Western society! Then one fine day, an alternative solution appeared in my mailbox. I received a very moving letter from someone who had read my concepts about transforming competition into partnership in *Dare to Connect*. His name was James W. Steen and he was a Canadian coach and former international level athlete.

In his letter, he shared with me part of a communication he had written to the Canadian Federal Minister responsible for amateur sports. It represented part of his ongoing effort to counter the damage being done to children and carried into adulthood as a result of the present-day obsession by their elders to WIN at all costs. He wrote of the need to restore the only values that he felt could justify the public funding for athletics. He said:

> "We see 8-10 year old children being screamed at while struggling against hills designed to break the backs of Olympians: 'GO Joey!' 'PUSH Joey!' 'WIN Joey!' 'You have to want it, Joey!' The little Joeys don't want it but scramble valiantly on without any technique or skill to offset the ebbing strength of their immature bodies. The shame of failure seems the only driving force. We have seen the highest levels of officialdom witness such nonsense, or more to the point—abuse—without taking the slightest notice. Their concerns are obviously in a different sphere. The mania to win can only translate into losing on all fronts."

Remember, these are words coming from a superior athlete with a true love of sports who still competes and coaches at levels ranging from children to high performance athletes at World Cups! He goes on to say . . .

"Sports, more than anything, can be a way for youngsters to learn that their competitor on the 'field of honor' is not their adversary, but their partner . . . and to learn that the object is not to beat her or him, but to bring out the best in both and grow together with generosity, honesty, loyalty and respect."

Stated in this way, competition is a wonderful thing, indeed. But as it stands, athletic competition (and we can also include competition in business, politics, education and so on) has become a sad mass of destructive behavior that comes from the lowest part of who we are. "Honor" doesn't even enter the arena. I'm sure you can cite instances where this is not the case but, in the larger picture, the spirit of mutual respect and caring seems to be lost.

It would be wonderful if we could transform the playing field into its potentially life-enhancing magnificence . . . a place where we can "bring out the best in both and grow together with generosity, honesty, loyalty and respect." But we seem to have a very, very long way to go in accomplishing this goal.

You may be asking, "Why is it so hard for us to see all forms of competition as a place for honor to emerge?" One of my favorite sayings which comes from the Talmud is:

"To a worm in horseradish, the whole world is horseradish."

Indeed, the whole of Western society seems to be immersed in the "horseradish" of our conditioning and we cannot see that there could be another way. In fact, of all the things I have ever spoken about in my workshops, my criticism of competition elicits the most confusion and disagreement. My students are so immersed in the horse-radish of "win at any cost" that they find it very hard to see the value of a field of honor.

It seems essential to me that we climb out of the horse-radish and see there can be another way. We need to learn how to transform the field of win-or-lose into a field of honor in all our endeavors. While we can't change the world (at least not immediately!), we can change the way we participate in the world. When we see (and teach our children to see) our "opponents" as allies, whether they are on the field of athletics or in business or wherever, the world takes on a different energy.

With a friendly challenge from a talented "partner", we become more focused on expanding our skills. We align ourselves—body, mind and Spirit—to bring forth the best that we have to offer. When this happens, we truly do become allies in helping each other improve our skills and the whole energy of the game of life is altered. Here, there need not be any loser. In this game, both can win.

I have heard tennis players saying they love to play with really good opponents. Win or lose, their game improves. Their opponents have become their allies. In this kind of arena, we play the game of life, not with obsession, but with a loving heart and a desire to expand to the best of our ability. To me, this is what the field of honor is all about.

Yes, we have a long way to go on this subject . . . and we must take a first step. But it is a step that needs to be taken for the good of everyone in Western society . . . and ultimately the world. James W. Steen has started the ball rolling for me, metaphorically speaking. I hope that he has started the ball rolling for you as well.

Adapted from *End the Struggle and Dance with Life*

13.

Ten Tips for Helping
a Man Open Up

Note: This one's for the women . . . but, men, you
can read it too!

WOMEN, DON'T FEEL FRUSTRATED when your
man doesn't open up. Instead, use his silence as an opportunity to explore new ways of empowering the relationship
and yourself. Here are some tried and true tools for
creating a safe space for closeness to occur:

1. *Change Your Expectations.* Understand that in
   Western society men are not trained to be verbal in
   the same way women are. Remember that men would
   love to open up but, as yet, do not know how to
   speak the language of openness. (But they're
   learning!)

2. *Notice His Attempts to Connect.* Even if they are not
   verbal, be appreciative of men's attempts to connect.
   These attempts include gifts, sex, telephone calls,
   reports of the day's activities, physical touching.

Notice these loving and caring acts and say "Thank you" a lot!

3. ***Learn the Beauty of Silence.*** Create a rich inner life so that you are not needy of your man to fill the silence. He may not be able to open up but you have to pick up the mirror and ask yourself what bothers you about the silence. Hmm.

4. ***"Send" Love.*** If you feel tension when no words are spoken, relax, focus your attention on your man and silently say the words "I love you" over and over again. You will feel your inner tension melt. And your loving energy will touch him with sometimes surprising results.

5. ***Notice How We Don't "Walk our Talk".*** While we say we want men who speak openly with us, too many of us still find the strong silent type attractive. And, when men do open up and talk about their fears or their sadness, or other things of a personal nature, we think of them as wimps! It's time we learned how to love the humanness of our men . . . and embrace them for it. That's walking our talk.

6. ***Hold Back Your Unloving Responses.*** Hold back the judgment, defensiveness, competitiveness and tone of superiority when your man finally does open up. These behaviors create immediate separation instead of closeness. These behaviors also reflect your own insecurity. It would be wise to investigate why you need to put another person down. (I certainly had to work on that one!)

7. ***Learn from Your Talks with Your Female Friends.*** Women don't talk to their men in the same way they talk to their female friends. Good friends tend to support each other, encourage each other and thank each other. When talking to your man, ask yourself, "If I were talking to my best friend what would I say? How would I react? How would I listen? How would I empower her?" Then do the same thing for your man. Relax, lighten up and be supportive . . . as you would like for him to be with you.

8. ***Remember, It's a Time of Transition.*** Women are often confused as to what they really want from men and from a relationship. Because of our confusion we send mixed signals. Mixed signals make men very confused . . . and confusion understandably creates very quiet men! It's time for us to once again pick up the mirror and ask ourselves "What do we really want?" Interesting question! (Of course, men are confused as well but this article is about us.)

9. ***Leave Some Space for the Men to Open Up.*** Some of us talk and talk and talk and talk. If this describes you, as it sometimes describes me, stop talking too much! When you create the space, his thoughts may be more forthcoming.

10. ***Have Patience.*** Things are slowly improving. First women had to learn the language of openness with other women. Men are now learning to be more open with other men. It's just a matter of time when we will be more comfortable being open with each other as well.

A final thought: We can't change men . . . as they can't change us. But we all have the power to change our own negative thoughts and expectations that makes connecting with each other very difficult. As we change our own behavior, we open the door for men to be more open with us. And who knows? We may ultimately find a "soul-mate" inside the man behind the mask! At least that's what happened to me.

© 2000 Susan Jeffers, Ph.D.

(You can learn much more about taking charge of your life and creating a deeper connection with men in *Opening Our Hearts to Men* and *The Feel the Fear Guide to Lasting Love*.)

14.

The "Schindler" in Us All

I DON'T THINK I WAS EVER as moved by a film as I was by *Schindler's List*.[1] I decided to see the film long after Steven Spielberg received his many deserved accolades for creating it. In truth, I hadn't intended to see the film. It was about the Holocaust, a subject matter I preferred to avoid. But thankfully something within me said, "See this film." And I am grateful that I listened.

There may be some of you out there asking, "Who is Schindler?" Very briefly, Oskar Schindler, at one point in time, was a shrewd, fast talking, womanizing, money hungry German man who initially turned his back on the horrors taking place during the Holocaust but who, little by little, evolved into a caring human being who continuously risked his life and spent every penny he had on successfully keeping 1300 of his Jewish factory workers alive. For this, he is admired by many.

As I pondered this powerful film over a long period of time, I came away with the realization that while, thankfully, few of us are ever faced with such extreme circumstances, the many faces of Schindler live within us all:

There is the "early" Schindler . . . the part of us that doesn't really care . . . the part that thinks we're entitled to more than everyone else . . . the part that is psychologically numb to the needs and cares of those around us and those far away . . . the part that uses others only for our own personal gain.

Then there is the "middle" Schindler . . . the part of us that is beginning to wake up, but is still a bit groggy. Our tendency is to know the truth but to look away. It's easier that way. We don't want to be reminded how uncaring our lives have been at times. We don't want to be reminded that there are those who look to us for help . . . and we often look away.

And then there is the "seeing" Schindler . . . the part of us that finally understands that we have a purpose in this world . . . that our lives have meaning . . . that we have been given the ability to make a significant difference in our own lives and the lives of others . . . and our beauty emerges.

I remember that after leaving the movie theater, I sat in my car and cried and cried and cried. I cried for the part of us all that sometimes gets stuck in early and middle Schindler . . . when we are not giving a helping hand to those who need our help. I cried for the part of all of us that sometimes get caught up in society's message that success is equal to making money, attaining power and status and looking good instead of caring, loving, touching and helping. I cried because so little has changed since the time of the Holocaust. The animosity between the races, sexes, cultures, countries and religions continues. There is hatred in the air as we hear people berating each other everywhere we turn. Oh, yes. Love is also in the air. But the voices of hatred too often tend to be much louder than the voices of love.

It seems to me that it's now time for the voices of love to get louder and louder and louder. We need to awaken the "seeing" Schindler within us all. We need to understand at the very deepest level of our beings that our lives make a difference . . . that our actions really do contribute to the pool of energy that defines this world. Too many of us do not have this understanding. It is clear that a change in how we think about ourselves will help us become a force of love and peace within our families, our communities and our planet.

To know that we really count is the most powerful and vital piece of information we can have. It introduces a whole dimension to our being—that of responsibility. Not to worry! A sense of responsibility that comes from a realization of our inner power is not a burden. It enables us to leave behind our frightened egos and jump to the highest part of who we are. It allows us to create acts of love that make us feel alive and joyful . . . even blissful. At such times, we know we have found that magical place within that we have been searching for our entire life. We have only to begin the Journey—one step at a time—to the best of who we are, and, with each step forward, we find ourselves a little bit closer to Home.

© 1999 Susan Jeffers, Ph.D.

15.

A Fateful Day
by Gerry Gershman

NOTE: I raised my children in New York City at a time when children of a certain age routinely played in the city parks and enjoyed other aspects of this great city without parental supervision. (For a variety of reasons, children don't enjoy this freedom in today's world.) When my son, Gerry, reached adulthood, he wrote about one particular experience which had a huge impact on his life. He gave me permission to share it with you. I think it is a story that will warm your heart.

It was in April, 1969 when something happened to change my perception about muggings and muggers . . . and everyone else in the world.

I was eleven and, as was common for other kids my age, I had been "mugged" at least eight or nine times by roving groups of young hoodlums. Usually these confrontations cost us no more than a few dollars, our bus passes and watches but it was all very scary anyway. I came to know the tell-tale look on their faces. I could smell trouble—it was an uncanny instinct—like I was somehow connected to this immaculate divining rod that sent a shock up my spine and engulfed me in fear, sweat and an acute sense of survival.

One day I was enjoying New York's Central Park with two of my closest friends, Tommy and Peter. We were playing our homemade version of stickball using tennis rackets. Another after-school episode in paradise. From over a hill I happened to notice a kid about seventeen years old approaching our carved-out playing field. Then I noticed three others, a little younger, approaching us from different angles. Being that our field was not exactly a thoroughfare, my astute sense of panic took over.

After a second of intensive eye contact with my buddies we knew the party was about to break up. We were outnumbered and these guys were way too big to run away from. We pretended to continue playing as if nothing was happening but like buzzing bees our stalkers knew we were shaking in our boots.

Two of the kids made a B-line towards Peter. Tommy was approached by the third. And the biggest of them all chose me as his target. I was petrified and in my usual manner I became very courteous and accommodating to this "monster" making sure I didn't do anything to upset him in any way. I remember once apologizing to some muggers that I didn't have more money than I did. I actually helped them evenly divide up my change. But this time I was wearing a nice watch, I had a few dollars in my pocket along with my bus pass and apologies were not necessary as I handed over the goods. My obsequious nature usually kept me out of more serious danger and this time it was no different.

Ultimately, the big guy signaled to the others that it was time to move on. They casually strolled off together knowing full well that there was nothing we could do in retaliation. As they disappeared over a hill, Tommy, Peter and I convened in the center of the field nervously recapping the events that had just taken place.

At that moment, I happened to glance over to the roadway that runs through the park and noticed a Jeep-like police car driving along. I didn't think I could catch it, but nonetheless I instantly bolted after it. The cop in the driver's seat saw me running and stopped the car. The words raced out of my mouth as I relayed the incident.

To my surprise the two cops told me to jump in and we were off and racing through the park over huge rocks, on pedestrian walkways, across the park roadway and onto the street adjacent to the park. I felt as though I was in a James Bond movie. My adrenalin was pumping. My eyes were keen as we searched for the muggers. Finally I spotted them. When we pulled up next to them they reflexively started to run but realized, as we had earlier, that there was no way out. We had won. It was over—or so I thought.

The cops got out of the car and rounded them up. I was watching this from the back of the Jeep trying not to let them see me—for I was responsible for their capture and I did not want them to know it. As the cops were leading them to the Jeep it occurred to me that these guys would be getting in next to ME! I was right. The four muggers and ME were all squeezed into the back seat! This was the worst nightmare I could have imagined! As the police car started to move, my eyes were riveted to anything outside the window. I was petrified that for some reason I would have to look at these guys. I didn't like this situation one bit.

Finally, the cops deposited the gang at the Central Park Precinct and drove me back to the park where my friends had waited. We all drove back to the precinct where a sergeant filled out a report as we described it. The gang was being questioned on the other side of the station, which was comforting to us. We didn't want to be anywhere near them! We were happy to find out that they had turned over all the stolen property to the cops.

After finishing our report, we were delivered to our respective homes where we told our story to our parents. They were all amazed and pleased that we had actually caught the muggers this time and that they were going to be brought to justice. We were pleased as well. The good guys won. We told everyone. We were heroes.

It was about six weeks after the mugging when the trial date was set and we had to appear in court to testify. My father volunteered to be the obligatory parent who had to accompany us. Tommy, Peter and I conjectured about the court process and what the outcome would be. The thought of seeing these guys again made us a bit uneasy about the whole thing.

Tommy and Peter met early in the morning at my house and, with my father, we all went downtown to the courthouse. We made our way to our designated waiting room—a 30 x 30-foot basement room filled with people as nervous as we were. We checked in with the court clerk and found seats on one of the ancient benches that lined this dingy depressing excuse for a room.

We sat. And as we waited, we looked around the room. What was everyone else doing there? Did they have great stories like ours? We made daring glances at the sullen faces, then conferred amongst ourselves as to what their respective fates were. We were wired. After an hour of waiting and getting more comfortable with our surroundings, time started to drag on. The courtroom deputy was calling cases at an alarmingly slow rate. It seemed like we could be there forever.

Then it happened. With his eyes, Tommy directed me to the front door . . . our muggers were walking into the room! We tried to become invisible. I alerted my father to the new situation. The clerk directed them to seats on the other side of the room. I felt like I was back in the Jeep in the park. We realized that these guys were going to wait in the same room with us and the only question was how long was this going to last. We noticed them . . . and pretended that we didn't notice them. Hours passed. I accidentally caught the eye of the mugger who had taken my watch but with lightening speed I turned away. Things couldn't have felt more menacing.

Finally, the court day ended and, much to our chagrin, our case had not been called. Everyone was told we would have to return the next day to resume our waiting game. This was not good. But, we had come too far and we were going to see it through. Of course, for us it meant we could take another day off school and that was a worthwhile consolation.

So on day two we arrived promptly, checked in, sat down . . . and waited some more. As the day lumbered on, we loosened up a little and started goofing around a bit. Of course, we were always aware of "the enemy" across the room.

At around three o'clock Tommy made the outrageous suggestion that we should go over and talk to them and we told him that he was out of his mind. Tommy wanted to know why we shouldn't talk to them. No response. Finally, he got up to go to the bathroom and on his way back he did the unthinkable . . . he talked to our predators! A minute later he returned to our seats and we were in shock.

Despite our disapproval, we inquisitively grilled him on the nature of the conversation. They had been friendly and apparently so was Tommy. They had exchanged hellos, joked about the endless waiting and Tommy said he would talk to them later. This was blowing my mind but I was interested in the new development.

The day ended and our case had still not been called. We had spent two eight hour days with no results. Tommy's mother offered to take over the custodial role for the next day in court. We were old hands as we checked in the following day and Tommy's mom was noticeably more uncomfortable than we were. When the gang showed up, we pointed them out to her. We also noticed many other familiar faces in the room. And we waited.

At one point on my way back from the restroom I walked right by the muggers and inadvertently caught the eyes of the gang leader. I tried to conceal the fact that I was shaking inside but his eyes were not so threatening and for a moment—just for a moment—I experienced him, not as a mugger, but as a person just like me. Nothing was said but something was buzzing inside me. What were these guys all about? My curiosity was aroused.

I decided that I, too, wanted to talk to the gang but I was too nervous to approach them. But I finally mustered up the courage and the three of us strolled over as if we just happened to be walking that way. It was intense. As we approached, Tommy blurted out some form of a hello. One of the younger guys responded. They seemed to be curious about us. But unlike us, they seemed to be fairly relaxed. The second gang member commented about the length of time we had all been waiting, which was now almost three days. This was my cue. I excitedly jumped in trying to initiate an exchange of thoughts.

We all concurred that missing school was certainly a blessing despite the tedious waiting game. They let us know that this happened all the time—that they were used to it. Mugging was a way of life for these guys. They told us many stories of their escapades. They told us they liked to wear loose-fitting khaki pants which made it easier for them to run from the police. I seemed to connect with the big guy, the leader, the one who had removed my watch from my arm six weeks earlier. We continued discussing the whole court process. We marveled at the dysfunctional bureaucracy and this became our bond. We talked about our families, our neighborhoods and our schools. Similarly, Tommy and Peter were deep in conversation with their former foes. We connected as we tried to under-stand each other. And for the first time, I realized that despite the travesty of waiting for three days in a dungeon of justice we had found a way to accomplish something really meaningful.

The day ended without our case being called and from across the room, we signaled goodbye to the gang as we made our way back to the subway and back home. My mother and father both decided to come back to court with us on the fourth day. Tommy, Peter and I were psyched. We had some serious drama happening and this was about ten thousand times more interesting than another day at school!

So the five of us went downtown the next morning. As my mother was taking in the scenery, we noticed our gang. Unlike any of the previous mornings we were totally comfortable as if we were seeing some of our old school buddies. In a very short time, we had abandoned my parents for the gang and were immersed in chatter about last nights TV shows, the Mets, movies and, of course, missing more school. They were into letting us know how cool and tough they were but I didn't really mind. I was struck by their total disdain for their teachers and education in general but I felt we were having this amazing cross-cultural exchange and my fascination overtook my usual judgmental nature. They were O.K. in my book. We had vastly different outlooks on life but at least theirs seemed original.

At one point, I started to realize that sooner or later we were going to be called into the courtroom and summoned to testify against our new "friends." Internally I questioned whether or not I should be responsible for getting them in trouble. We had developed a rapport and I had a sense of compassion for them.

In their world they had made some decisions that we would never have made but in the environment from which they came, those decisions did not seem so ridiculous. I learned they had fears, loves, uncertainties, hearts and heartaches . . . and I felt truly connected to them. But we had come too far to back out of the court proceeding now and, even though our relationship had been totally transformed, we still had to see it through. And, after all, we had been mugged!

After lunch, I started playing gin rummy with the gang leader. In the back of my head I couldn't help reminding myself that I was soon going to be testifying against him. And the strange thing was that I knew he understood. It was part of the deal. At about 3:30 that afternoon our case was finally called. The moment of truth had arrived.

We gathered our day's possessions and were escorted by the deputy into the courtroom. We were seated on opposite sides of the room and we watched as a cop read the outline of the original police report. The proceedings would have been totally nerve racking four days earlier but now it was only the formality that seemed so foreboding. I was hoping that I wouldn't have to be called to the stand. Of course I was. I was asked to identify the gang. It was brief but I avoided all eye contact and felt like a heel.

Our muggers pled guilty. After some deliberation the judge declared his sentences. He told the big guy that this was serious business. And his already very long police record would be duly marked. The other three were advised that they were on the wrong track and it better not happen again. Months of conversations and worrying. Four full days of waiting and missing school. Parents forced to miss work. A slap on the hands. And they were free to go. THAT WAS IT!!!

But for me, it was so much more. The experience had transformed me. Prior to this experience, I would not have believed that I could have developed a relationship with the muggers . . . but I did. They were not "them" anymore. We had all been in this together and we were still in this together. The dark veil had been lifted and I felt a great sense of accomplishment, completion and trust. While the "powers that be" created a potentially dismal situation, we were able to create a beautiful experience. The walls of separation had come down. It was one of the most profound experiences of my life.

We waved goodbye to our new friends for the last time. On our way, we passed the eternal waiting room, and I took a last look at the people still sitting around. Their faces looked different. I saw their humanness and felt a sense of camaraderie. I wanted to meet them all and tell them everything was going to be all right . . . that it was already all right.

FOUR MONTHS LATER: I was standing in front of the Hayden Planetarium waiting for the light to change and a big guy around seventeen years old approached me, grabbed my shirt and demanded all of my money. Amazingly, I wasn't afraid. I knew he was just another guy beneath all his defiant behavior. I paused, I looked him in the eyes and, in a friendly manner, I let him know that I would give him everything I had but I wanted to know what he was going to do with the money. I was talking to him as a person and not like a mugger. He repeated his demand several more times and I repeatedly told him I was interested in his life and just really wanted to know what he wanted to do with the money. He looked at me with surprise and confusion. Finally, he let go of my shirt and told me to forget it. Our eyes connected once again and he walked away. A few minutes later, I realized what had just happened. I was in his heart . . . as he was in mine.

This was a story I told over and over again in school, to my parents, to Tommy and Peter and to anyone who would have listened. I still tell it.

I was never mugged again. In fact, neither was Tommy or Peter. Maybe it was luck. But I believe I had lost my divining rod to danger and it was replaced by understanding and a sense of compassion. I was no longer a victim waiting for a mugger. After all, it's hard to punch a man in the face when he is smiling at you. Of course, there are exceptions. There's always some lunatic out there waiting to randomly hurt or kill someone but, after my experience, I had the sense that I could handle any situation that came my way.

One year later I was at a friend's house watching television with his family and news about the latest casualties in Viet Nam came onto the screen. My friend's father commented how the commies were our enemies and we should kill them all. He was convinced that they were going to get us if we didn't get them first. And at the age twelve, I noticed that I had compassion . . . even for him.

My perfect little world had been small and now it was huge . . . and it was still perfect.

© 1995 Gerry Gershman

16.

Tears of Joy in the Supermarket

"TEARS OF JOY IN THE SUPERMARKET, Susan? What are you talking about?" Trust me when I tell you that there was a time in my life when I used to walk into a supermarket and be bored out of my mind. Food shopping was a horrible chore I had to do before I could get to something I wanted to do. Then one day, I learned the concept of "looking deeply." I decided to give this concept a real test by practicing it in the supermarket. I figured that if it works there, it will work anywhere!

So the next time I went to the supermarket, I gave it a try. Trust me when I tell you that I was astounded by the power of this simple tool. There I was standing in the aisle with tears rolling down my eyes as I "looked deeply" and was able to focus on the miracle of it all. I have never walked into a supermarket again with dread; rather, I always walk in with a wonderful feeling of awe and anticipation.

I know you must be curious. So let me show you how this "looking deeply" works so that your next visit to the supermarket will be one of joy as well . . .

As you walk through the door, stop for a moment and survey the rich array of goodies from which you can choose. Trust me when I tell you that there are few countries in the world that have such abundance.

Then, as you fill your basket with a dozen eggs, a loaf of bread, salad fixings and a whole basketful of other goodies, look more deeply and notice the huge variety you have to choose from—so many kinds of bread, so many kinds of greens, so many kinds of cereals, so many kinds of desserts. The richness of it all is staggering.

As you focus on the abundance in your basket, look a little more deeply and focus on the money you have to pay for your purchases. Even if you can't buy everything you want, you can buy enough to sustain you. (Given the number of overweight people in our society, most of us buy more than enough to sustain us!)

Next, look even more deeply as you focus on the farmers who grew the greens that gave you your salad fixings and raised the chickens that gave you the eggs and grew the grains that gave you the bread and cereal. Focus on the bakers who baked the bread. Focus on the drivers of the trucks, captains of the ships and pilots of the planes that transported all these riches and made them so available to you.

Then look even more deeply as you focus on the staff that is there to serve you; some of them have been up since very early in the morning to set up the displays in a way to please you. Focus on the people who took a risk and invested their money to create a market to provide you with such sumptuous fare. Focus on the people who built the building that is home to the market.

Then look even more deeply and focus on those who created the roads that allowed you to drive your car to this place of wonder . . . and those who manufactured the car that gives you so much mobility.

Then look as deeply as you possibly can and focus on the ultimate Source of it all . . . God, the Force, the Universal Light . . . whatever it is for you, that created the air, the sun, the water, the earth, that makes all growth possible. One can't deny the miraculous rhythm and flow of it all.

We could be there all day and couldn't look deeply enough to encompass the astounding miracle before us. When you look at the supermarket in this way, it is a monumentally large gift that we have been given. Now can you see how moments of boredom even in the supermarket can be turned into exquisite moments?

Let me put the icing on the cake. A dear friend, Martha Lawrence, once gave me the following poem by Emily Dickinson, which says it all . . .

As if I asked a common alms
And in my wandering hand,
A stranger pressed a Kingdom
And, I, bewildered, stand.

We went to the market for a tomato, and when we looked deeply "a stranger pressed a Kingdom" in our hand.

I suggest you begin looking deeply at everything you do in your everyday life—driving your car, working at your office, taking a vacation, reading a book, watching television, gardening, cleaning your house, caring for loved ones and so on.

As we make looking deeply a habit, we are constantly reminded that in so many aspects of our lives, we have been handed a Kingdom. And with this realization comes a wondrous sense of gratitude and joy. Yes, the power of this simple tool will amaze you . . . as it most certainly amazed me.

© 1996 Susan Jeffers, Ph.D.

(This tool plus many more tools for creating a joyful life can be found in *End the Struggle and Dance With Life*.)

17.

"Why Hasn't He Called?"

NOTE: This article was written many years ago when I was single . . . and VERY insecure about men. It reflects the behavior of so many single women of my day. And I suspect that, even though women have grown so much over the years, this is one area that still needs a little work. But if we can lighten up and learn to laugh at our insecurities, we are definitely on the right track!

I HAVE A CONFESSION TO MAKE. I'm an addict—a telephone addict, that is. It's not that I have a need to talk on the phone. No, it's more subtle than that. I have a need to wait by the phone . . . with the hope that HE might call. Ever since I was about fourteen years old, I've needed that daily fix from my love-du-jour. Even if whoever-he-was-at-the-time didn't say he was definitely going to call, I would run home with the hope that he MIGHT call. And there I would wait . . . and wait . . . and wait.

I still wait. Different man . . . same wait! Nothing much has changed. Even now, as the minutes tick away, I can feel myself sinking lower and lower into a deep depression when HE doesn't call. And then, the phone rings. Exhilarated, I pick it up. "Oh, it's only you," I say in a disappointed tone to my girlfriend at the other end of the telephone line. I wonder how many times I've offended her with this warm greeting. "I can't talk now. HE might call." (Unfortunately, we didn't have access to multiple phone lines in those days!) I suspect she understands.

At one point in my life I said, "This has got to stop." So the next time, he (whoever HE was at the time) said, "I'll call you tomorrow", I cleverly, (I thought) said, "No, I'll call you." I felt such a sense of relief knowing I wouldn't have to wait by the phone the next day. My ordeal was over. I had found a way of licking the habit. WRONG! Would you believe he wasn't home when I called?

So I spent the evening dialing instead of simply waiting. Once I let the phone ring 100 times. In a one room apartment, one has to assume he could pick up the phone from anywhere on the second ring! What was I waiting for? What could I have been thinking? That he'd pick up on the 56th ring? Pathetic! After that disaster, I decided to go back to waiting, rather than dialing all night. At least I could do something constructive with both my hands free—like painting my toe-nails.

I went on a holiday once where there was no phone. I was like a crazy person—such withdrawal symptoms. (We didn't have cell phones then either!) I pondered if women in primitive tribal villages have the same addictions . . . I mean, do they sit around all night and wait by their drum?!? Anyway, after a few days, it got a little easier. I began to feel whole again.

It then occurred to me that perhaps the answer was to have my phone removed from my apartment. Knowing there was no way to reach me, how could I possibly feel rejected? Wrong again. I realized I would only be trading addictions. The poor postman would be assaulted each day as he delivered the mail. "What do you mean there's no letter for me! Are you sure? Maybe you better look again." . . . and so on.

I then thought that perhaps an answering machine would be the solution . . . so I made the investment. (It was early days where answering machines were concerned.) The day it was installed, I went out with the girls with a free mind knowing my trusty little machine was doing the waiting for me. As I opened the front door, I was exhilarated to see the red light beaming on the machine telling me someone had called. My exhilaration turned to upset as I pressed the button to hear my message. Yes, someone had called . . . and hung up without leaving a message. Is there no justice? Shall I call and ask him if he called?

So what is behind this franticness to connect? Is it a need to know I am loved? Absolutely! Is it that I distrust what he's up to without me? Absolutely! And it's something much deeper than that. It feels as if the relationship will be over unless the connection is made. And so far, I've been right!

The only thing that suggests to me that I am not totally insane is that my addiction is shared by all my female friends. "I must run home now. I'm expecting a call from my boyfriend." (Again, this was the pre-cell phone era.) This sentence has cut short many a delightful evening out. Yet, I can't remember any one of us ever running home to wait for a phone call from another girlfriend! Nor can I ever remember getting upset if a girlfriend says she'll call and I don't hear from her. I simply figure that she got tied up and couldn't call. No problem. We'll connect tomorrow . . . or whenever. I don't feel less cared for or rejected.

But when HE says, "I got tied up", I feel terrible. You see, if the situation were reversed, I can't imagine myself in a situation where I couldn't pull myself away for a moment or two to make a phone call to him. Somehow, somewhere, I'd find an opportunity to connect—even if I needed to send a message by carrier pigeon! I wouldn't let him down. If I said I'd call, I'd call! He can't understand what's the big deal. He's right. What IS the big deal? But then again, he doesn't know the anguish I go through waiting for him to call . . . or does he. Hmm.

In any case, this has got to stop. I'm going to break this ridiculous habit. No more waiting around. No more heartbreak. I don't need his phone call to prove I'm loveable. You'll see. In a few weeks, I'll be totally cured. A new woman. The time to start is definitely . . . tomorrow. Right now I must rush home. I'm expecting a call from . . .

18.

The Surprising Power
of Affirmations

I AM A STRONG BELIEVER in the power of affirmations. They have been and continue to be remarkably healing to me. As I repeat certain affirmations to myself over and over again, I can feel my negative thoughts being replaced by a wonderful sense of confidence, peace and possibility.

What is an affirmation? As I am using it here, an affirmation is a strong positive statement telling us that "All is well" despite what the negativity in our mind is telling us. What is truly surprising is that the frequent repetition of this simple statement has the power to relax our bodies, quiet our minds and allow us to see the brighter side of life. Amazing.

There are many reasons why affirmations may be so powerful. I believe that one of these reasons is that, while the affirmation is usually only one sentence in length, it embodies so much more. It embodies a deeper and wider meaning that invites a healthy way of thinking and acting . . . which partly explains why affirmations can be so effective in improving the quality of our everyday lives. Let me give you a few examples:

Affirmation
I TOUCH THE WORLD WITH LOVE WHEREVER I GO.

Deeper and Wider Meaning

I radiate a sense of love everywhere I go. With a smile, a helping hand, a sparkle in my eyes and an open heart, I embrace all with whom I come into contact. As I give the best of who I am to family, friends, work, community . . . and to myself, I am filled with a sense of joy. I have so much love to give. Yes, I touch the world with love wherever I go.

Affirmation
I LET GO OF MY NEED TO CONTROL EVERYTHING AROUND ME.

Deeper and Wider Meaning

I release my fear about the outcome of all situations in my life. I realize that the pathway to peace lies in my doing my best in all things and then letting go of the outcome. As I let go, I affirm my trust that whatever happens is for my highest good and the highest good of all concerned. No matter what happens, I will look for . . . and find . . . the great learning that can come from all situations in my life. In so doing, I am filled with a sense of peace. Yes, I let go of my need to control everything around me.

Affirmation
THE QUALITY OF MY LIFE DEPENDS ONLY ON ME.

Deeper and Wider Meaning

I blame no one as to how I am feeling today. I have the power to act and react to all situations in a healthy and self-affirming way. Step-by-step, I let go of what no longer works in my life and embrace those things that bring me a wonderful sense of self. As I do, I watch the quality of my life getting better and better. Yes, the quality of my life depends only on me

Affirmation
I LIGHT THE FIRE THAT WARMS MY WORLD.

Deeper and Wider Meaning

I take responsibility for reaching out and inviting others into my life. Pushing through any fear of rejection, I don't wait to be invited, I invite; I don't wait to be complimented, I compliment; I don't wait to be thanked, I thank; I don't wait to be loved, I love. In this way, I am a force of comfort and joy to all those around me. I notice how good I feel when making others feel welcomed and loved. Yes, I light the fire that warms my world.

Affirmation
WHATEVER HAPPENS, I'LL HANDLE IT!

Deeper and Wider Meaning

Within me, I have the power to handle anything that ever happens to me. I will learn from it all, grow from it all, and use it all as a means to reaching the best of who I am.

Every situation in my life offers me the opportunity to become a more powerful and loving human being. I have nothing to fear. I will always find the strength within me to find my way . . . and to find the good that ultimately comes from all that happens in my life. Yes, whatever happens, I'll handle it!

Affirmation
I SMILE AS I RECOGNIZE THE MANY BLESSINGS IN MY LIFE.

Deeper and Wider Meaning
Right now, I choose to put stressful thoughts aside and let the abundance in my life fill my being. I focus on the many things, big and little, that fill my life with joy . . . my family, my home, my friends, good food, the sunshine, my ability to help the world in my own way . . . and all other aspects of life that nourish my soul. In so doing, my world becomes a beautiful place in which to live. Yes, I smile as I recognize the many blessings in my life.

Affirmation
I AM POWERFUL AND I LOVE IT!

Deeper and Wider Meaning
As my strength grows and grows, I love the feeling of joy that overcomes me. It makes my heart sing knowing I have so much to give, so much to do, and so much to experience. With each step I take, I am reminded of the purpose of it all . . . to give love and receive love . . . and to be a meaningful part of creating a better world. Yes, I am powerful and I love it!

Affirmation
I PICK UP THE MIRROR AND ASK, "HOW CAN I BE MORE HELPFUL HERE?"

Deeper and Wider Meaning

Instead of worrying about the petty details of my life, I shall focus on my ability to help those around me in some way. I know that in so doing, I become a winner instead of a whiner. I win self-respect and the many other rewards that come with being a force for good. There is so much to do in this very needy world and I feel blessed that I can do my part in improving the lives of others in any way I can. Yes, today, I pick up the mirror and ask, "How can I be more helpful here?"

From these few samples, you can understand why a simple affirmation can have such a positive effect on our lives. An affirmation is not just a sentence; it represents a way of life. It is a means of taking ourselves from the lowest part of who we are to the highest . . . a place of power, purpose and love.

I have made it a habit to start repeating an affirmation that fits the moment whenever my negativity gets in the way of my feeling good about life. Soon I can feel the negativity abating and a sense of power, purpose and love filling my being.

As you can tell, affirmations have made a wonderful difference in my life. I believe in the power of affirmations so much that:

- I created a series of affirmation books and tapes.[1]
- I include a daily affirmation on my website.[2]

- I co-authored *I Can Handle It*, a book of 50 stories for parents to read to children based on one of my favorite affirmations "Whatever happens, I'll handle it!"[3]
- And while I mention them in most of my books, I created a "mini-course" on how to use affirmations in *Feel the Fear and Beyond*.[4]

If it sounds as though I am trying to get you hooked on affirmations, I am! They are one of my favorite tools for improving my experience of life and I am so happy to be able to share what I have learned with you.

Understand that as you learn more about affirmations and start using them regularly in your own life, you will find that some will work for you and some won't. It takes some experimentation. I certainly have my favorites. Trust your gut as to whether an affirmation is appropriate for you.

As you begin using your favorite affirmations, you will notice that little by little, the "habit" of thinking negatively will be replaced by the "habit" of thinking positively . . . powerfully . . . lovingly . . . and peacefully. Certainly, that has been my experience.

© 2002 Susan Jeffers, Ph.D.

19.

Why All the Teenage Violence?

TEENAGE VIOLENCE seems to be increasing in today's world. If it were not such a serious and confusing matter, it would be very comical watching all the "experts" on television yelling, fighting and pigheadedly pointing a finger at one special area in society that they insist is the SOLE reason for the alarming increase in teenage violence today.

One blames parental neglect; one blames the easy availability of guns; one blames violence in the media . . . or films . . . or television . . . or video games . . . or the internet; one blames the mind altering drugs carelessly prescribed by doctors; one blames the lack of God in our lives; one blames the hate and alienation promoted by religion; one blames the cruel and inhuman teasing of teenagers by other teenagers; one blames genetic factors; one blames an inadequate school system . . . and on and on and on. Crazy-making, isn't it?

Let me un-crazy your mind and give you an explanation that works for me and makes all the pieces of the jigsaw puzzle fall into place. Many years ago, I was introduced to the term "critical mass", a term coined by physicists in the 1940's to determine how much uranium was needed to start a chain reaction leading to an atomic explosion. Can you see where I am going with this?

Could it be that in recent years, we have unwittingly provided enough ingredients in society to start a chain reaction leading to a new kind of explosion . . . an explosion of teenage violence? Of course, none of us intended to do this, but we succeeded beyond our wildest nightmares!

Could any one thing have enough power to start the chain reaction leading to the horrors of teenage violence as so many so-called experts proclaim? Probably not. But add all the above factors together and that's exactly what we've created.

Think about illness in the body. I suspect that in most cases, the germs won't do it alone, a bad diet won't do it alone, lack of sleep won't do it alone, lack of exercise won't do it alone, stress and fatigue won't do it alone, and the list goes on. But as, one by one, we keep adding negativity to the body's defenses, there comes a moment when a critical mass is reached and the body can no longer hold its own. It is then that sickness ensues. What it takes to reach this critical mass varies from person to person, from age to age, from situation to situation. It is almost impossible to predict who, when and why anyone gets sick, because so many factors enter into the picture. Nothing does it on its own, yet all are involved.

And so we are cautioned to lighten the body's load of negativity—to keep our distance from others who are ill, to eat well, to sleep seven or eight hours a day, to exercise, to find ways to relieve our stress such as meditation, yoga, vacation time and so on. And if we do all of this, the load on the body will lighten and it is more likely that our immune system will remain strong enough to protect us from illness.

In the same way, one thing alone probably will not create a surge in teenage violence, but add up all the negative factors confronting teenagers today and, inevitably, some will commit violent acts towards themselves and others. Again, what it takes to reach this critical mass leading to violence also varies from person to person, from age to age, from situation to situation. And again, it is almost impossible to predict who, what and why anyone reaches this violent state, because so many factors enter into the picture. Nothing does it on its own, yet all are involved.

Given all of the above, the answer to today's teenage violence . . . and violence in general . . . seems crystal clear. We must reduce the amount of negativity to stop the chain reaction leading to the explosion of teenage violence. How do we do this? One way is to stop all the finger pointing. Blame is a powerless and alienating form of behavior. What do we do instead? We pick up the mirror instead of the magnifying glass to figure out how each one of us in our own personal circle of life can decrease the critical mass leading to all the violence in today's world. The critical question becomes "What can I do to stop the hatred and alienation in my own thinking and in the thinking of others?"

This means that whether we are film-makers, gun haters or gun advocates, parents, religious leaders, creators of video games, recording artists, teachers, teenagers, or whoever . . . we have to pick up the mirror and begin to see where we can actively reverse the growing weight of negativity enveloping our society today, which ultimately is creating more violence . . . and then—step-by-step—

begin reversing the process. Can you feel the weight of negativity lifting as you imagine this process occurring?

And ultimately, if a large enough number of us do our part, we can create a new critical mass . . . one that creates a chain reaction leading to an explosion of love in this world. There is no question that the power of the collective consciousness is awesome. It's time we begin pointing this awesome power in the right direction . . . toward a world of caring and connection instead of judgment and alienation.

Yes, the finger pointing has to stop and our taking responsibility has to begin. If not, the violence will definitely continue . . . or worse, increase. It is up to each and every one of us to make a difference in the problem with violence in today's world. We do that by finding new ways of spreading our love in the world in any form that it takes. And by making our collective voices heard. We all need to take that first step.

I ask you (as I ask myself): "What is your first step going to be? What are you planning to do—step-by-step—either in your home, with your children, at your job, in your community, in politics . . . anywhere that is appropriate for you . . . to erase the violence and create more love?" The actions you and I take can make all the difference in the world.

© 1999 Susan Jeffers, Ph.D.

20.

What Is Our Purpose?

I WAS RECENTLY ASKED a very interesting question . . . "What do I consider to be the purpose of people on this earth?" The truth is that I don't have a clue . . . nor, in my opinion, does anybody else. How can we know? Our mortal minds simply cannot know what I love to call "The Grand Design," the great mystery behind it all. We can speculate, but how can we "know"? The good news, and I am always looking for the good news, is that . . .

Since we don't know the purpose of our life on earth, we have an incredible opportunity to create our own purpose. And if we are wise, we pick one that brings us joy and satisfaction . . . instead of one that degrades our sense of self.

Makes sense, doesn't it?

Over the years, I've "tried on" many purposes. Some didn't work and some worked for a time. With much experimentation, I learned that I am happiest and most joyful when I am . . . 1) LEARNING how to put more love and trust into all my thoughts and experiences and then . . . 2) TEACHING what I've learned to others. Hence, I consider "learning and then teaching about love and trust in whatever form that takes" to be my purpose. That makes everything in my life "grist for the mill". As I learn from my experiences—good or bad—I can't wait to tell you what I've learned . . . which has the added advantage of making all my bad experiences good!

I notice that when I am off-purpose in my personal or professional life, which happens at times, it is a guarantee that I will lose my sense of joy. As I re-focus once again on my self-created purpose, the joy returns. I stop worrying about the petty things that are driving me crazy and I am at peace once again.

So your task is to experiment and see what kinds of actions bring you great satisfaction. It is different for everyone, of course. Some possibilities are:

Being kind to others in all that you do.
Helping the world to be more beautiful
in any way you can.
Easing other people's pain.
Teaching children to be more loving.

We all need to find our own sense of purpose by asking, "What brings me great joy and satisfaction?" Then, the important step: Find the many ways you can act relative to the answers you hear.

I believe that in order to find true joy and satisfaction, we have to become Higher Self thinkers . . . people who are in touch with the best of who we are. And then we have to put that "best" out into the world in anyway we can. There is no question that when we make our purpose one that comes from the Higher Self, we are on the right track for creating inner fulfillment. Of course, we all seem to sink into Lower Self thinking every once in a while . . . that seems to be a human trait we can't escape. However, when we know our Higher Self purpose, we always have something wondrous to return to. It's a beautiful process.

A word of caution: When asking the question, "What is my purpose?" some of you may hear the answer "making money." There is nothing wrong with making money. In fact, I love making money! It is when making money is devoid of Higher Self thinking that we lose our way. I know so many rich people who have no sense of Higher purpose and they derive very little joy. I also know people who make their money in a way that hurts and deceives other people. Again, they are unhappy as they haven't gotten in touch with the best of who they are. Thankfully, there are those who make money and who are Higher Self thinkers . . . and they truly help the world in so many beautiful ways. They can't help but feel good about their lives and who they are as human beings. You get the picture.

Maybe you are having trouble finding your own sense of purpose? If that is the case, I'll lend you mine. I'm convinced that most people would find joy in the learning and teaching about love and trust in whatever form that takes. Certainly it works for me.

I love to delve into such interesting topics as this. It reminds me of the endless conversations I use to have as a college student, sitting around with friends into the wee hours of the morning. But in the end, there are no proven answers to such questions; hence, it is wise to create our own answers that feel good within the depths of who we are as human beings. And, of course, we must allow others to create their own answers that feel right for them. That's the real advantage to having questions that have no answers! Nobody gets to be right . . . or wrong! Hmm. There seems to be an important lesson here!

21.

No Victims Here:
Taking Responsibility for Our Lives

IN MANY OF THE SELF-HELP BOOKS you read (including mine) you are told, "Take responsibility for your life!" You may be wondering, "What exactly does this mean?" As I explain in *Feel the Fear And Do It Anyway* . . .

1. *Taking responsibility means never blaming anyone else for anything you are being, doing, having or feeling.* Never? But this time, you say, it really is his fault (or her fault, or the boss's fault, or my son's fault, or the fault of the economy, or my mother's fault, or my father's fault, or my friend's fault . . . .If I missed anyone or anything, just add it to the list). Until you fully understand that you, and no one else, determines your REACTION to whatever happens in life, you will never be in control of your life. *Remember that when you blame any outside force for any of your experiences of life, you are literally giving away all your power and thus creating pain, paralysis and depression.*

2. *Taking responsibility means not blaming yourself.*
I know this sounds contradictory, but it is not.
Anything that takes away your power . . . or your
pleasure . . . makes you a victim. Don't make yourself
a victim of yourself! It is important to understand
that you have always done the best you possibly
could do, given the person you were at any particular
point in time. Now that you are learning a new way
of thinking, you can begin to perceive things differently and possibly change many of your actions and
reactions. It is all simply part of the learning process
—the process of moving from pain to power—and it
takes time. You must be patient with yourself.

3. *Taking responsibility means being aware of those
circumstances in which you are not taking responsibility, so that you can eventually change.* It took
me years to realize that the place where I played the
role of victim most often was in my relationships
with men. I remember spending many evenings with
my girlfriends, complaining about the grief the men
in my life were causing me. It was a Moan and Groan
Society. The payoff was that we didn't have to create
our own happiness —we could simply blame men for
not giving it to us. Relationships are only one area in
which we give away our power. It is important for
you to look at all other areas of your life as well to
determine where you are not taking responsibility.
Your clue will be any signs of anger, upset, blaming,
pain, self-pity, envy, helplessness, joylessness or
disappointment. This is not a complete list, but you
get the idea. Whenever you feel these symptoms,
determine what you are not doing that is causing you

to feel that way. You will be surprised at how easy it is to locate the area in which you are abdicating responsibility.

4. *Taking responsibility means silencing the Chatterbox.* This is the little voice inside your head that tries to drive you crazy—and often succeeds! It's the voice that heralds doom, lack and loss. The good news is that there are very effective ways to get rid·of this kind of negativity—for example, by "outtalking" the Chatterbox with constant repetitions of positive thoughts, such as . . .

> **"I am a powerful and loving person."**
> **"It's all happening perfectly."**
> **"I relax and I let go."**

When you notice that your Chatterbox is casting you as a victim, commit to replacing it with a loving voice. You don't have to associate with enemies—not even the ones within yourself! And, by the way, once we silence the negativity of our Chatterbox, we really begin to enjoy being alone.

5. *Taking responsibility means being aware of payoffs that keep you "stuck."* Payoffs are the rewards we receive from NOT changing something we don't like about our lives. Once we understand payoffs, our behavior makes much more sense to us and we are able to take positive action. Let me give an example:

Jean felt horribly "stuck" in her job. She viewed herself as a victim. Her Chatterbox played the "if only" tape: "If only the job market were better; if only I had better skills . . . " What was really keeping Jean at her job? What were the payoffs? Jean clearly had become very comfortable as a victim. By not searching for a new job, she didn't have to face possible rejection. Although she hated her job, it was easy. She knew she could handle it. And the job was relatively secure. Once Jean realized she was staying because of the payoffs, and not because of her "if only's" (a bad job market and her lack of skill), she was able to break away and find a new job.

Yes, hidden payoffs have great power in your life. But they are not so difficult to discover once you realize that they exist. If you can't find them, ask a friend to help. You might be surprised to learn that your friends know more about your motives than you do!

6. *Taking responsibility means figuring out what you want in life and acting on it.* Set your goals, then work toward them. We might find other goodies along the way that we prefer to do, but as long as we realize it is all our choice, we are taking responsibility. What is most important is our decision to enjoy the process despite how it all turns out.

7. *Taking responsibility means being aware of the multitude of choices you have in any given situation.* It is so important to realize, as you go through each day, that at every moment you are choosing the way you feel. When a difficult situation comes into your life, it is possible to say to yourself, "Okay,

choose. Are you going to make yourself miserable or happy?" The choice is definitely yours. For example:

—Your friend decides not to go on the trip you had planned together. You get angry. Or you understand that she has her reasons for not going, and you find someone else to go—or you go alone and have a ball!

—Your husband drinks too much. You spend all your energy scolding him or trying to change him. Or you attend Al-Anon meetings and learn how to change yourself by reacting to the situation in a healthy way.

—You are sick with the flu and have to miss a very important business meeting. You are sure that your absence means the end of your career. Or you realize that you have limitless ways of creating a successful career for yourself.

Can you see how the choice is yours? You have the power to place yourself on the "up" side of any situation. Keep in mind that this way of thinking is not meant to excuse inappropriate behavior on the part of others. It simply allows you to have a more satisfying life.

These are just a few tips to help you look into your life and see where you are not taking responsibility. Learning to take responsibility for your experience of life is a long process that requires practice. I'm still working on it every day of my life. The point is simply for you to begin. You will feel better immediately.

You can start by seeing if you can get through one week without criticizing anyone or complaining about anything. I can almost guarantee that you will have a very silent week! Each time you experience upset, be conscious of the other emotional alternatives that are available to you. Make it a game . . . and laugh a lot. Remember these two words and say them to yourself often: "I choose."

(For more on this subject, go to *Feel the Fear And Do It Anyway*.)

22.

A Love Story

I WROTE THIS ARTICLE as a tribute to my husband, Mark Shelmerdine, who is the most loving and caring man I have ever known. At the time of this writing (2001), we have just celebrated our 16th wedding anniversary and I wanted to share with the world just how blessed I feel. Our amazing relationship makes my heart sing.

How did we come to such a wonderful place? Through a great deal of learning and growing, we have both come to realize that everything we did wrong in our first marriages, we are doing right in this one . . . and it shows. Let me give you a small sample of some significant differences between my first marriage and this one. They may be of help on your journey toward love:

In my first marriage, I never appreciated anything my then-husband did for me. Now I keep my eyes wide open and notice even the littlest of things that Mark does to make me happy. And then I let him know how much I appreciate every one of his acts of caring. The words "thank you" keep coming from my lips . . . and his.

In my first marriage, I was always angry. Why? Being young and stupid, I didn't realize that I was supposed to pick up the mirror instead of the magnifying glass and take responsibility for my own experience of life. I kept waiting for my then-husband to fill me up with joy and happiness and all good things. Over the years, I wised up. By the time I married Mark, I understood that it was up to me to make myself happy. As a result, blame does not define my feelings for Mark; love does.

In my first marriage, I didn't feel as powerful as I now feel. I have learned over the years that power and love go together. Without power, neediness prevails. Mark and I have both grown to feel powerful within ourselves and, as a result, we have a tremendous amount of love to give to each other. To me, that's equality in the best sense of the word.

In my first marriage, I lived the fairytale dream of "'till death us do part." Now I take it one day at a time, knowing that if we don't nourish the now, there can be no "'till death us do part". Without nourishing the now, it is more likely to be "'till divorce us do part." Nourishment of our relationship is an important part of our every day lives.

In our first marriages, we were both very foolish. Age has brought both of us great wisdom when it comes to love. We never stop the learning and we keep practicing the art of appreciation, thanks, giving, caring, receiving and loving. We have discovered that as each of us gives, the thanks come back in multiples, which sets up a cycle for a magical relationship, indeed.

With each anniversary, we make it a practice to re-affirm our wedding vows . . . a beautiful way to remind both of us of our commitment to each other. Sixteen times, we have held hands, looked into each others eyes, listened to an audiotape of our original ceremony, and proudly and joyfully said our "I do's". And each year the vows become more and more meaningful.

We have reaffirmed our vows alone or with our beautiful family and dear friends. We have reaffirmed our vows on the tops of mountains, by the water's edge, in beautiful restaurants, on the deck of our beautiful home or wherever the Spirit has moved us.

Wherever and with whomever we affirm our vows, the significance of the ceremony never changes. It is to renew our commitment to love, honor, and certainly not to "obey", but to encourage each other to be the best that we can possibly be. That feels great. That feels right. And without question, it creates the basis of an incredibly strong and healthy relationship.

So thank you, my darling Mark. Whenever you walk in the door, the whole room lights up for me. I love you more than words could ever say.

A September 11th Trilogy

The previous article entitled *A Love Story* was my website article for the month of September in the year 2001. It was meant to be there for the entire month . . . but then September 11th happened. A seemingly new world emerged as we sat in front of our television sets watching the World Trade Center and the Pentagon being attacked. I felt moved to replace *A Love Story* with an article entitled *Am I Dreaming?* which is a picture of New York that was sent to me by e-mail from two people who were actually there. The first one came from Ashley Jacobs who is now my loving daughter-in-law. The second one came from a dear friend, Roseann Yaman. I believe these two e-mails will touch your hearts.

Two other relevant articles follow in this trilogy. The first of these, *The Healing Face of Love*, consists of my observations of the United States after September 11th. The title of the second speaks for itself . . . *My Tribute to New York*. Having lived and worked there for many years, I know it intimately and I am always awed by its magnificence. Perhaps it will give you a picture of a New York that you have never seen before.

23.

Am I Dreaming?

Part I

Tuesday, September 11, 2001 9:39 AM
Sent by Ashley Jacobs
Subject: Am I dreaming?

Hello:

I just wanted let everyone know that Guy and I are OK. We live about twelve blocks from the World Trade Center and have (or rather, had) a perfect, majestic view of it from our rooftop. I walked out the door to go to work on this sunny, bright blue-sky morning and witnessed a vision I never imagined possible in real life. There was a massive, gaping hole on the top floors of one of the World Trade Towers. Flames were bursting through the windows, and huge blackish gray mushroom clouds filled the sky.

Through one of the Towers, you could see bright blue sky intertwined with bright orange flames through the opposite side of the building where massive holes ripped through it from the explosions and the crashes. I could practically touch the smoke clouds, and I could certainly taste them as I walked to work. People, human beings, were jumping out of the World Trade Tower buildings with only a hope and a prayer that their lives would be saved, but knowing deep inside that their life on earth was soon to be over. Blaring sirens filled the streets. And you could not help but ask yourself, "Am I dreaming right now?"

People were gathered on street corners (every street corner), some crying their eyes out, some taking photos, and some just in absolute awe at the sight. Loud news reports filled the air from open cars and trucks. People were talking on the streets and later in my office, as they remembered the people they know that may have been in the buildings and tears filled their eyes.

We had clients on the 105th floor of the first Tower, who we have not heard from and may tragically never hear from again.* Our hearts go out to their families and close friends, who like us, must be terrified, but we are praying for their health and safety and for some miracle that may have saved them. Some miracle, any miracle—like they happened to be late for once, or they called in sick, or something. (People from our office were supposed to be there for a meeting, but thank God that the proposed project wasn't ready yet so we had to postpone the meeting! In this case, tardiness literally turned out to be a life-saver!)

For most of you that know me, you know I am not one for sending big group e-mails, but this is too important for me to ignore. This is the most tragic moment I have ever witnessed, and hope to ever witness, in my lifetime.

*And tragically none of them ever was heard from again.

I do not send this to bring sorrow and report the tragedy that must be filling your TV and radio waves, but I send this to remind everyone how important each moment is and how so much is unpredictable in this truly crazy, mad world.

Remember to make every moment count because it's the only moment that is truly certain and is truly sacred. Remember to tell those you love, you love them. And feel lucky you have them and they are safe. I know I feel very lucky right now for the wonderful people who fill my life and who are safe.

My heart,
Ashley

Part II

Sent: Tuesday, September 11, 2001 7:06 PM
Sent by Roseann Yaman
Subject: We're OK

Dear Friends,

It's been a devastating day, but thank God, Peter and I are OK. I was calling Long Distance to find out how my father, who is in the hospital, was doing, and Peter was working uptown on 56th and 8th Ave. The World Trade Center is way downtown, about three or four miles from our apartment.

I looked out of our 5th floor bedroom window, and I could see the black smoke billowing in the sky. That was when the first plane crashed. I sat glued to the TV when I saw the second plane crash into the North Tower. I think my mouth dropped to the floor when I heard about the Pentagon. Then . . . I got really scared. I had no idea if we were under enemy attack, or if the incidents were isolated. I don't think I've ever taken a shower as fast as I did after that news. Truth is, I didn't want to get caught in my nighty in the event that I had to leave the building!

It took Peter 2½ hours to get home. Public transportation was practically at a standstill, and we didn't think the Subway (if it was running) would be a good idea. Thinking of germ warfare or fire, he opted to walk or sit on an air-conditioned bus for a couple of hour while it crawled.

My cousin Chris was visiting from Rochester last week and left just last night. She and I were on the ground floor of the South Tower just last Thursday and Friday, buying theater tickets. We also lusted over a Krispy Kreme shop in the Plaza, but decided to pretend we didn't see it. As Peter always says, "Timing is everything," and I can't tell you how happy I am that we were down there last week and not this.

I stood on a very long line at the supermarket since I hadn't done any food shopping in a week. We ate out every night while my cousin was visiting. Standing behind me was a young man that worked just a block away from the World Trade Center, and he had stopped at that same Krispy Kreme shop this morning. He told me that he had ordered a coffee and walked outside. He actually saw the plane hit! He dropped his coffee and ran for cover. He lives in New Jersey and there's no way for him to get home, so he's staying with a friend, and is very grateful to be alive.

I also spoke with an attorney neighbor of mine who works in the Wall Street district. I think he was still in shock. He saw the second Tower collapse, and he said that what he saw didn't seem real. He too voiced his gratefulness.

People say that New Yorkers are very hard people with little feeling. Not so when it comes to a crisis. You've never seen such a huge group of people unite when help is needed. I can't tell you how many people I know who were on their way to donating blood and helping others in any way that was necessary. It's quite a sight to behold. It's like one big family. Streets and sidewalks were jammed with people walking. Those that could get home, walked. Those that couldn't were offered some place to stay. I overheard a woman in the meat section of the supermarket offering her two pull out sofas to the butcher and a person that fills the cases. And they hardly knew one another!

Cars were bumper to bumper and even the police cadets were directing traffic. All of my neighbors were out at the playground sitting on the benches and talking about what had happened. I guess we all needed to talk about it. The emotions expressed were from surprise, to sorrow, to anger, and a few other emotions in between.

Well, tomorrow is another day, and I think that we will all be feeling something even deeper. We've all lost something, and some of us will have lost someone that we know. I dearly hope that this is the end of a terrible tragedy and not the beginning of something else.

In the meantime, we send you all our love and we want you to know that however you have touched our lives, we are that much richer.

Peter and Roseann

24.

The Healing Face of Love

AS I WRITE THESE WORDS, many of us in the USA and throughout the world, consciously or unconsciously, are grappling with the aftereffects of the horrific terrorist attacks on the World Trade Center in New York and the Pentagon in Washington. Initially, our eyes saw only the horror of the pain and loss of life experienced by so many innocent people. But, in a remarkably short time, this sense of horror was superseded by an awesome feeling of love, unity, caring, giving, helping and a profound determination that we shall learn and grow from it all.

In my entire life, I have never experienced such an unimaginable sense of love and togetherness. I witnessed so many ordinary people acting in such extraordinary ways. I thought to myself, "Wow! This is what a nation truly united in love actually looks likes! How spectacular!" I was not alone in my thoughts.

Yes, I know these intense feelings of unity will diminish as time passes. Who knows what the future holds? But I also know that at some level we all have been transformed by the vision of having witnessed and experienced such intense expressions of love . . . so many heroes giving so much. It is something we will never forget.

Young and old "gave themselves away" as they got involved in the task of helping—young kids with their lemonade stands, entertainers, businessmen, sports figures, the medical establishment, and the ordinary people who became extraordinary as they gave of themselves to raise money and to help those in need.

Then there were the firemen, policemen, emergency workers and many volunteers risking—and sometimes losing—their lives to rescue others. Some beautiful beings actually sacrificed their lives rather than leaving others—sometimes total strangers—to die alone in the towering buildings that soon became rubble. The magnificence of it all takes your breath away. The words "Thank you" are on all of our lips as we learn the true meaning of "giving".

An unimaginable horror? Yes. An unimaginable outpouring of love? Yes. The Zen Master Masahide once said . . .

Barn's burnt down—now I can see the moon.

I wonder were he alive today and observing the happenings on and since September 11th, if Masahide would have stood there in wonder and said,

The buildings are gone—now I can see the love.

Yes, many have died; at the same time, the love has risen. We actually have a modern-day Masahide. The wonderful Jon Stewart, anchorman of The Daily Show on

Comedy Central, came back on the air after the September 11th attack on America with the following:

> "The view from my apartment was the World Trade Center and now it's gone. They attacked it. This symbol of American ingenuity and strength and labor and imagination and commerce and it is gone. But you know what the view is now? The Statue of Liberty. The view from the south of Manhattan is now the Statue of Liberty. You can't beat that."

The symbolism is breathtaking.

We can only guess if more acts of terrorism will follow. Maybe yes; maybe no. But as we focus on the process of learning and growing from it all, we actually become less afraid, knowing that, despite what happens as a result of this atrocity, we will come out of it stronger, and more alive with the possibility of becoming a more meaningful part of the world . . . each of us in our own way.

© 2001 Susan Jeffers, Ph.D.
(From *Embracing Uncertainty*)

(These are difficult times and in *Embracing Uncertainty* you will find 42 exercises for helping you handle all that has happened—and all that will happen—with a sense of power, love and possibility.)

25.

My Tribute to New York

I LOVE NEW YORK. I lived in Manhattan for many years. I left almost 20 years ago when the great adventure called LIFE beckoned me to many new places . . . but a part of my heart has always remained there. My husband, Mark, and I visit there quite often, and it always feels like I am coming Home.

What do I love about New York? I love the energy I feel just walking down the street. I love the crowds. I love the melting pot kind of feeling. I love the togetherness. I love the sense of possibility. I love the Spirit of New York. Yes, I LOVE NEW YORK!

In a strange kind of way, I feel safer in New York than any other place that I have ever visited or lived. And September 11th hasn't changed that. In a way, September 11th has enhanced my feeling of safety. The people are more closely knit, the vigilance is greater, and the Spirit shines even brighter.

I visited Ground Zero . . . the spot where the World Trade Center once stood. Even with tradesmen selling their souvenirs to curious visitors, I felt it was a sacred spot. I bought one of the souvenirs . . . a book of astonishing photographs that depict the dramatic events of September 11th and the aftermath. You see . . . I don't want to forget. I don't want to forget about the courage and the love that was exhibited that day. I don't want to forget how precious and fragile life is.

Even though I haven't lived in New York for many years, I feel I "know" the people who live there. For ten years I was the Executive Director of New York's Floating Hospital, an actual ship that welcomed the poor aboard and offered them all kinds of health services . . . along with an exhilarating trip around the Manhattan harbor. I always loved it when we approached the Statue of Liberty. I can only have imagined the sense of intense hope immigrants felt when this symbol of WELCOME appeared before them.

As a result of my job, I was able to touch the Soul of New York. I touched the hands and hearts of rich and poor alike. I touched the Spirit of giving. I touched the Spirit of community. Yes, it's strange that one can live in a place with millions of other people and have a sense of community.

I loved the poor who embraced me. Even though they were struggling with many issues, they were strong and giving and loving. They taught me much about laughter and joy. I loved the rich who cared so much about helping the poor. I loved the many who volunteered—rich AND poor—to help others who were facing great difficulties in life.

The New York firemen displayed their heroism in a magnificent way on September 11th. But I knew about their sense of giving and caring many years before. I always could count on a number of firemen to appear on their days off to give assistance in any way they could aboard The Floating Hospital. Every time I saw these courageous volunteers approaching the ship, I breathed a sigh of relief. I will never forget their strength and generosity. They represent so much of the giving Spirit of the people in New York City.

I know many of you are thinking, "Susan, we know it isn't ALL great in New York City." And you are right. In fact, I have always perceived New York as having the best the world has to offer . . . and the worst! But I think it is just this mixture that gives New York its vibrant energy and excitement. Thankfully, I was able to hear, touch, see and feel so much of the best that New York has to offer.

On a recent trip there, Mark and I availed ourselves of the myriad things New York has to offer a visitor . . . great restaurants, great theater, great shopping and on and on and on. It was a splendid holiday. But unless you have lived among the people of New York as I have, it's hard to really "know" New York. I always advise friends who visit there to do what I always do: enjoy all it has to offer, but take a moment to embrace and inhale the amazing world of beauty, strength, diversity and love that inhabits this wonderful city.

I know this all sounds like a paid advertisement for New York City! But trust me when I tell you this comes straight from the heart. So . . . THANK YOU, NEW YORK . . . for being the city you are. And thank you for giving me some of the most beautiful experiences that life can offer.

© 2001 Susan Jeffers, Ph.D.

26.

Do You Have a "Fribbish" in Your Life?

NOTE: After the previous three articles, I had an intuitive sense that a little bit of humor was needed. So I pulled out my "funny file" and found some thoughts I wrote down many years ago . . . 1983 to be exact. I hope I put a smile on your face.

I HAVE A DILEMMA that I'm sure many of you will recognize. I am living with a man, but I am not married to him. (That's not the dilemma—even my mother has accepted the arrangement.) My problem has to do with introductions. I defy any of you out there to find the word that tells it like it is. For example, everybody understands "spouse" or "wife" or "husband", but I can find no word that applies to my situation when it comes to those tricky introductions. And believe me, I've tried . . .

"This is my, uh, friend." *So is my dog, but it's hardly the same.*

"This is my man." *That's obvious from the suit and tie.*

"This is my partner in life." *People want to know what business we're in.*

"This is my steady companion." *That sounds as if he answered my ad in the newspaper.*

"This is my boyfriend." *I stopped using that term when my acne cleared up for the last time.*

"This is my love." *Closer . . . but still not it.*

I think you get the point. The word does not exist. The English language is far behind the times.

It seemed to me that the only sensible thing to do was create a word that truly worked. After much pondering, the word that inexplicably came into my mind was "fribbish." You say you've never heard the word before? Precisely. It had to be a totally new word, devoid of any other meaning.

You're skeptical. You say, "Fribbish sounds funny". Sure it does. But if you think about it, I'm sure that the first time the word spouse was used everyone thought it sounded funny. You say, "Fribbish reminds me of rubbish". Sure it does. But, I'm sure people were once reminded of "louse" by the word "spouse." But trust me when I tell you that after using it for a while, it will sound perfectly natural and delightful and you'll wonder how you managed without it.

To help you get through the "sound barrier", just do as I say: Repeat "I'd like you to meet my fribbish" one hundred times and you'll notice that it starts to feel really right. Don't take my word for it. Try it.

Now, the question remains: "How can we make fribbish a household word?" For this I need the help of all you out there who have a domestic arrangement similar to mine. You're introducing him (or her) at a party. You simply say, "I'd like you to meet my fribbish, Mark (Joe, Bob, or Henry, or whatever). "Your what?" will most likely be the reply. You answer, "You know, my fribbish—the love of my life with whom I live." Not wanting to appear stupid, the person you're addressing will probably respond with, "Of course, your . . . uh, fribbish."

I know it will take time for it to catch on, but if we persevere the day will come when fribbish takes its rightful place in the dictionary, between "friary" (defined as a convent for friars), and "fricassee" (defined as dishes of pieces of chicken or meat, fried or stewed and served with rich sauce). Fribbish will be defined as "either member of a cohabiting, unmarried loving couple."

Oh, by the way—and this will shock you—as I peruse my trusty dictionary, I see the word "wife". Would you believe that this old edition of The Concise Oxford Dictionary actually gives its first definition of wife as "an old and rustic or uneducated woman"? I'm so relieved. I'm sure fribbishes will be much more highly regarded.

I can sense you are still feeling skeptical, and I can understand that. You'll probably feel a little silly the first time you introduce your fribbish, but you'll get used to it eventually. And when your mother's acquaintances ask, "Has your daughter (or son) finally found a husband (or wife)?", she can reply with a new sense of smugness and pride, "No, but she has found a wonderful fribbish." How great that is!

EPILOGUE: Many years have passed since I wrote the above article and I still can't find the word fribbish in the dictionary. We must all work together to rectify this situation. Onward! I might add that a few years after these words were written, I traded in my title of fribbish for that of spouse. I must admit that my dear mother did breathe a great big sigh of relief. I've learned that given a choice, a mother usually will prefer a spouse to a fribbish for her child.

27.

Letting Go of the Little Things

IT IS A STRANGE FACT OF LIFE that we let little—very little—things take away our precious peace of mind. How silly is that? In his wonderful book, *Joy Is My Compass*,[1] Alan Cohen describes his great moment of awakening when it came to letting go of trivial things in his life that tend to drive him crazy. This moment didn't come upon him on the top of a great mountain or at the edge of a vast ocean. No, his moment of awakening came to him at McDonald's! (There are many paths to awakening!)

He reports that from the minute he walked into McDonald's for a quick lunch, he was miserable. He remembered someone telling him there was sugar in the French fries. He imagined the presence of preservatives in the apple pie. He lamented the preponderance of noisy kids disturbing the whole environment, and on and on and on. Nothing was right. He vowed he would never return. But, then, as he sat there in what he called "the smog of my own thoughts," the voice from his Higher Self came through loud and clear. It asked him a profound question that made all the difference . . .

"What if this were all alright?"

He gasped, "What do you mean . . . alright?!? This is terrible!" His Higher Self answered . . .

"What if nothing around you holds any power to make you unhappy?"

What a concept! What a breakthrough! All of a sudden, Alan Cohen saw everything with new eyes. He looked at the boisterous kids and decided their laughter and shouts reflected their joy. What's wrong with a little joy in the middle of the afternoon? He decided a little sugar and preservatives wasn't going to affect his ability to love. He decided that everything that was previously annoying him was totally alright. He said . . .

"Something happened to me when I let it all be OK. I felt relief. My heart opened. I was at peace. I had found the answer to being there. I had found the answer to all of life. Just let it be."

With this realization, he got in line for some more French fries and apple pie, which, he concluded, was what they serve in heaven! And he basked in the wonder of letting it all be alright.

After I read Alan Cohen's story, I thought about all the little things in my life that I was constantly obsessing about . . . getting the right table in the restaurant, the weather, the stock market, the traffic, points of view that were different from mine, other people's behavior, getting everywhere on time. And so on. What a struggle!

What if any table I got was OK? What if the weather was perfect exactly as it was? What if my money in the stock market was irrelevant to my sense of security? What if the delays in traffic were just part of the scene? What if other people's opinion had nothing to do with my happiness? Or their behavior? What if life would go on joyfully even if I arrived at an appointment a little bit late? What if all that little stuff was OK? What a freedom! Then I would be "wearing the world just as a loose garment" instead of struggling to make it all different than it is.

So much of our struggle with life has to do primarily with minor things in life. The big things often pull forward an incredible sense of power and inner knowing. I had breast cancer many years ago and I handled it beautifully. I made it a triumph instead of a tragedy. By way of contrast, I got a very bad hair perm three weeks before my present marriage. Did I make that a triumph? No way. You would have thought my world was coming to an end. Even after the wedding, I was upset for months until the frizzy hair finally grew out.

Does this make any sense on a Spiritual level? Absolutely not! My Higher Self could care less about my hair. It's hard to believe my Lower Self cared so much, but it did. Had I known what I know today, I would have been in a much better position to say to myself . . .

Let go. Let peace. Let joy.

As I look at my laughing Buddha sitting on my desk, I now understand that one of the reasons he is always laughing is that he already knows that everything is alright! I think all of us should paste stickers everywhere we can see them, that say, "What if this were all alright?" It would help to remind us to pull ourselves out of the negativity of our Lower Self and lift us to the freedom of our Higher Self.

So think about the many little things that cause upset in your life. Getting a dent in your new car. Forgetting to buy something at the supermarket. Sitting in the airport for two hours because the plane was delayed. Rain when you had invited people over for a picnic. It's at these times that we really need to take a step back and asked ourselves that profound question . . . "What if this were all alright?" Yes, we do what we can to change what is not working in our life, but for those many little things we can't control, letting go, letting peace and letting joy is the heavenly way to go.

As an exercise, I suggest you write down all of the situations in your life that are causing you struggle and ask yourself the same question about each situation . . .

"What if this were all alright?" Each time you ask this question, take a deep breath and relax. You will experience a momentary feeling of peace. Do this over and over again until just the asking of the question is associated with a deep breath and a feeling of relaxation. And as you go through each day, notice where you are trying to control everything around you. Add it to your list and keep asking yourself the question, "What if this were all alright?"

If you think about it, what I am talking about here is simply a shift in focus. Why do we always look at what's missing instead of what's there? Why do we always look at the bad, instead of the good? Why do we always focus on the ugliness instead of the beauty? When we focus on what's missing, or what's bad, or what's ugly, we are operating from the level of the Lower Self. Why not rise above the Lower Self and see what the world looks like from the Higher Self?

For example, what if instead of focusing on the lousy table at the restaurant, we focused on the wonderful company, the luxury of having someone else cook our meal, the abundance of having enough money to pay for the meal, the blessing of good health to be out and about on a beautiful evening, and on and on and on. The table might still be lousy, but 99% of the evening is wonderful. Why focus on 1%?

We can create this shift in focus in all areas of our life that bring us upset. The truth is that blessings surround us all the time. That shift in focus isn't a delusion. In fact . . .

We are deluding ourselves when we focus on the bad!

Read that again! So when that lousy table comes up and there are no others available, you say to yourself, "Yes the table may be lousy, but look at all that is wonderful in this situation. How blessed I am!" Indeed, when life is seen in this way, we are a step farther in conquering our control addictions and there is very little that can take away our peace of mind.

I know it takes a lot of practice to reach a "let go" state of mind, but the one thing I can assure you is . . . I'll be practicing right along with you!

© 1996 Susan Jeffers, Ph.D.

(Adapted from *End The Struggle And Dance With Life*)

A Surprising Look at Violence Against Children

I wrote the following two articles to present a picture of violence against children which you may not have seen before. You may agree or disagree, but you know the rule: *take what works for you and let the rest go.*

28.

Do Parents Need to Panic?

THERE IS NO QUESTION that parents today walk around with heavy hearts when confronted with what looks like an increasing level of violence against children by perpetrators who seem to come from nowhere. The tendency to over-protect is a natural response. But one can argue that over-protecting our children is not a good thing . . . for parents or for their children.

Words of comfort come from Mary March, Director of the National Society for the Prevention of Cruelty to Children (NSPCC) in the UK. She tells us on the NSPCC website (www.nspcc.org.uk) that, while the recent deaths of young people is frightening, indeed, parents shouldn't panic. She states, "We have a duty to our children to remain rational, to allow our children to play outside, independently, so they can develop as ordinary children, understanding how to recognize and deal with risk."

I agree. I think we do a disservice to children when we hold on too tightly. When they are over-protected, it makes it very hard for them to learn the vast amount of strength they hold within . . . strength that ultimately allows them to know they can handle all that happens to them in life. One can argue that by over-protecting our children, we are putting them at greater risk, as they never learn how to protect themselves.

Ironically, there are statistics that show us that . . .

In recent years, the amount of violence perpetrated by outsiders has gone DOWN. However, the publicity regarding children's abductions and murders has gone UP . . . significantly.

This publicity is both a blessing and a curse. As a blessing, intense media coverage makes it easier to track and find abductors of innocent children. This brings comfort. As a curse, it keeps reminding parents of the dangers that could befall their children. This brings upset.

Understandably, all this publicity about children coming into harms way is creating what one observer has called "helicopter Moms." They hover over their children, which unfortunately prevents children from growing. I suggest that to ease this situation, parents keep reminding themselves that, yes, there is the possibility of harm coming to their children—*there always was and there always will be*—but they need to creatively find that delicate balance between letting their children explore on their own and keeping watch over them. That is today . . . and has always been . . . the greatest challenge of raising children.

I watch my younger friends being made to feel guilty if they don't hover over their children. In today's world, it takes a strong parent to go against the grain and stand up for what may be best for their child! We have to remember that our purpose is to help our children become independent and well-functioning adults. Hanging on too tightly stunts their growth and makes it hard for them to experience their inherent strength.

Can something happen to our children as we give them more latitude? Yes, of course, something can happen. But, as we are finding out, something can happen to them when they are lying in their own beds! Ultimately, we have to take a deep breath and let go. We have to keep reminding ourselves that beyond a certain point we have little control over what happens to our children. But what we do have control over is our *reaction* to it all. Just as we have to teach our children that they can handle whatever happens to them, *we have to teach ourselves that WE can handle whatever happens to them!* This way of thinking is our greatest safety net.

For inspiration we need only look at one of our great "heroes" who not only handled the loss of his child, but who had the strength and wisdom to help the world as a result of it. I speak of Marc Klaas, father of twelve-year old Polly who, in 1993, was abducted from her home in Petaluma, California and murdered. I point out how Marc Klaas was devastated when this happened, but he was able to turn his despair into hope for himself and many others.

With no prior media, political, or public speaking experience, he learned how to affect legislation and fight for children's issues. Ultimately he founded the Polly Klaas® Foundation, which has helped so many others deal with the terror that is experienced when a child is missing. Marc Klaas has created so much good from a deeply tragic experience. It gives us a greater peace of mind to know that we all have the power to create good from whatever happens in our own lives.

Letting go is probably one of the hardest things we can do as parents, but we must learn how to let go if we want to help our children discover how incredibly strong they truly are. Again, we need to find that delicate balance between letting our children explore on their own and holding on too tightly. Finding that balance is not an easy thing to do . . . but who ever said raising children was easy?

Something to think about: Mary March also stated that . . .

"Sadly, hard as it is to understand, we must never forget that the greater danger to the lives of our children lies with the very people who are supposed to keep them safe from harm and abuse—their parents and care-givers."

She is talking about the UK. The same is true in the US. And to break it down even further, government statistics in the US reveal that . . .

Only 2 to 3% of reported violence toward children under the age of 8 is perpetrated by care-givers while a whopping 65 to 83% of reported violence toward children under the age of eight is perpetrated by MOTHERS!

Are you shocked! Read on to see why this is so . . . and why mothers in today's world desperately need relief in caring for their children.

© 2002 Susan Jeffers, Ph.D.

29.

Why Mothers Need Relief

MY LAST ARTICLE WAS WRITTEN to help parents deal with the recent spate of violence against children by perpetrators who seem to come from nowhere. I ended the article by pointing out that according to government statistics in the US at the time of this writing, 2 to 3% of reported violence toward children under the age of eight is perpetrated by care-givers, while a whopping 65 to 83% of reported violence toward children under the age of eight is perpetrated by mothers![1] Given these horrific statistics, we all need to be aware of the intense frustration and exhaustion many mothers feel as they care for their young children.

Let me begin by reminding you of the day an au pair was accused of shaking a baby to death. The cry that went out was, "Mothers, go home! Don't go to work and leave your child in the hands of care-takers!" Given the above statistics, you can see why this cry of "Mothers, go home" might be considered irresponsible and/or uninformed advice to be giving mothers.

I don't know where this mythology of mother-as-saint came from, but it's time to explode the myth. Mothers are human. And in their humanness, there are times when they need help taking care of their children . . . whether it's in the form of nannies, child-care facilities, relatives, mothers pooling their efforts to substitute for one another, or mothers and fathers having more equitable responsibility in the raising of the children. Telling mothers that they should be the sole care-takers of their children, especially when they are infants, seems to me to be asking for trouble.

I will wager that most mothers, even those who adore parenthood, have, at some moment in time, had thoughts of hurting their children when their patience was running out. Most mothers do not act on these destructive thoughts, but unfortunately there are those who cannot control themselves and do physically lash out at their children. (It isn't that fathers are less capable of violence; it's that they normally spend less time with their children and, as a result, their rate of "eruption" is lower.)

I don't know what the statistics on child-abuse were years ago, but I suspect they were more positive. Hillary Rodham Clinton hit the nail on the head when she said that it took a village to raise a child. Years ago, there was always someone there to help when things got tough. For mothers today, the village is gone. As a mother sits alone in her home sometimes exhausted, sometimes bored, sometimes resentful, sometimes angry, she doesn't have someone's arms to hold her child until she has a little rest, a little pleasant diversion, and she pulls herself together again.

Therefore, if mothers were to listen to the "guilt-gurus" out there who insist that a mother should be the sole care-giver of her child for the first year or beyond of a child's life, I do believe that the risk of maternal violence being perpetrated against the child is greatly increased.

What makes the matter worse is that there seems to be a "conspiracy of silence" in today's world that makes it difficult for distraught mothers to tell the truth about their despair. They are afraid of being considered a "bad" mother. As a result, what is hidden in the closet of the world of the nuclear family is the large number of stay-at-home moms who are frightened that they will cause bodily harm to their children . . . or themselves. As one mother told me as I was interviewing her for *I'm Okay . . . You're a Brat*:

> "It's like after a while, with all the shrieking and screaming until all hours of the morning, I'd have such thoughts as, 'You could end this.' 'You could kill him.' 'You could jump off the terrace.' And there's the hormonal imbalance after a baby. My baby is two years old and I don't think my hormones are normal yet. To this day I still have these feelings."

I don't think anyone would disagree that this mother should not be the sole care-taker of her child . . . but she is. Unfortunately, she believed the guilt-gurus who told her she should go home to "bond". So she quit her job, became the sole care-taker of her child and is wondering what it's all about. Because she quit her job, she has no money for help in the form of other arms to hold her child. Nor do she and her husband have available cash to even enjoy a romantic dinner out together or a movie once in a while. This does not sound healthy to me.

Another woman told me:

"If you would have told me that I would have basically been going out of my mind with boredom and loneliness, I wouldn't have had a child. The truth is, I am so afraid to be alone with my baby."

And another:

"When my child was born, I was young, inexperienced and she had colic. And I thought I literally could kill her. One day I called my husband. I screamed, 'You have to come home. I am afraid I will kill this kid. I am out of my mind.'"

It is important to know that these thoughts are not unusual for full-time moms, the sole care-takers of their children. You might be thinking, "Oh, Susan, come on! I never heard mothers talk like this before." No, you probably haven't. There aren't many in today's society (where guilt is born with the baby) who have an easy time announcing they want to harm their kid! The conspiracy of silence zips most mouths shut. In fact, most of the mothers I interviewed told me they have never expressed their true feelings to another soul. On the surface, these women present a picture to the world of composure and happiness at being parents . . . but underneath a cauldron of dissatisfaction brews.

We live in a society that professes that motherhood is the ultimate fulfillment. And for some women, it is the greatest fulfillment. But there are many others who wonder where they were when those loving-being-a-parent genes were being handed out. For the latter, parenthood has turned out to be mentally, physically and emotionally exhausting. Sadly, they are ashamed to tell the truth of their feelings and they suffer alone.

Emotional and physical violence of varying levels happen often when our sanity is compromised with the unrelenting responsibilities of parenthood. One mother admitted that her son was frightened of vacuum cleaners and when he was in his walker, she used to deliberately "go after him" with a vacuum cleaner while he screamed with terror. One mother remembers slapping her child uncontrollably when he wouldn't stop screaming. Another remembers slamming a wall and wishing it could be her child. Are you beginning to get a sense of how damaging, even deadly, parenting-without-relief can be? And how damaging the conspiracy of silence is to all concerned?

THE DESPAIR THAT FULL-TIME MOTHERS SOMETIMES FEEL SHOULD BE SHOUTED FROM THE ROOFTOPS!

What I am saying here needs to be taken very seriously. Most first-time moms in today's world of the nuclear family are novices. And to hand all the responsibility and unrelenting demands a child brings into this world to a novice is asking for trouble. I don't care if this first-time mom is 20, as I was, or 40, as many new mothers are today, the responsibilities and demands can be overwhelming if there is no one there to help. Mothers need relief. And the fact that today's guilt-gurus are telling Mom to be the only care-giver for the first year or more of a child's life could spell disaster.

Let it be understood that mothers are, for the most part, very loving beings who adore their children and would do everything they could to help them grow up to be healthy and happy adults. As I said earlier, mothers are also human; they can explode when they have reached the limits of their patience. To always have helping hands available when they have reached this limit can be a life-saver—literally and figuratively.

I have been asked, "What would you tell mothers today?" I would tell them the following:

Don't let anyone dictate how you should or should not raise your child. For the sake of both you and your child, do what creates within you a wonderful sense of fulfillment. And we are all fulfilled by different things. If you feel fulfilled staying home, that's wonderful. If you feel fulfilled finding interests in the outside world, that's also wonderful. Many studies show that children who are exposed to multiple care-takers do just fine, in fact, better in certain areas.

If you need help, ask for it. Parenthood is difficult in itself; don't make it more difficult by suffering in silence. We've all seen the results when a dutiful mother loses her ability to cope. Remember: We can take proper care of our child only when we ourselves are physically and emotionally healthy. Honor yourself . . . and your child will reap the benefits in more ways than you can imagine.

I trust that in a few years, the conspiracy of silence will truly be broken as more and more people speak out. It is already happening. When the conspiracy of silence is broken, parents will feel free to talk openly about their difficulties in raising their children and they will feel free to create their own version of a "village" so that when times are tough, help will be at hand. At such a time, I believe that the amount of violence perpetrated by mothers against their children will thankfully go down . . . and down . . . and down. When that happens, we can all breathe a sigh of relief.

© 2002 Susan Jeffers, Ph.D.

(For much more on this subject, read *I'm Okay . . . You're a Brat.*)

> NOTE: I knew when writing *I'm Okay . . . You're a Brat,* I would be severely criticized, particularly in the US where parenthood is sacrosanct and I was right . . . I was severely criticized! But I believed from deep within me that many people needed to hear my message; therefore, I was totally prepared for all the criticism.
>
> What I wasn't prepared for (and what filled me with joy) were the poignant messages of thanks I received personally and in a number of reviews. A number of new mothers thanked me for literally saving their lives as, prior to reading my book, they were feeling suicidal. They were having a difficult time handling their negative feelings toward their new-born babies. But when they realized that many mothers in similar situations shared the same feelings, the terrible burden of guilt was taken off their shoulders. Just as importantly, they realized that there are many ways to create a fuller life for them-

selves so that they could better enjoy their time with their babies. I want to say to these women who contacted me, "Please know that your feedback has meant so much to me. I thank you from the bottom of my heart."

30.

Advice from Your Relationship Coach

For a brief moment in time (two months), I was pleased to serve as the Relationship Coach for an Internet site. Unfortunately it went out of business. I hope it had nothing to do with my being their Relationship Coach! Actually, I thought I did a pretty good job. I leave that for you to judge. What follows are some of the questions and my answers that appeared on the site. I had a great time answering these questions and who knows? Perhaps I'll take on the role of Relationship Coach once again if the opportunity arises. I'd enjoy that. I hope you enjoy the following:

Mary asks:
My partner seems angry and withdrawn, and his behavior towards me is unpleasant. I don't know why, as he won't talk about it with me. I find it very difficult to communicate with him. How do I break down this great wall that he's built around himself—or should I give up on him and move on?

Susan answers:

Mary, it sounds like a very lonely relationship! You ask, "How do I break down this great wall that he's built around himself?" The answer is, "You can't. Only he can." The only wall you can break down is your own.

If this is new behavior on his part tell him firmly, and with as much confidence and love as you can muster, that he has to let you in on whatever his problem is or you will have to leave. Suggest that you both go for counseling. If he just isn't interested in solving the problem, it's an "I love you and I'm leaving" kind of scenario.

If he has always been this way, pack your bags. It's definitely time to move on, as it's doubtful that he'll change. One of the most telling lines from my book, *Opening Our Hearts to Men*, is, "There's nothing as unattractive as footprints on the face." And it sounds as though, in his own way, your guy is definitely "stepping on your face." You deserve to give and receive the best. Being in this relationships allows you neither.

But there should be no blame here. It's all about learning and growing. This is a wonderful opportunity for you to take a look inside and find out why you were attracted to such a negative person in the first place. Sometimes we have to kiss many frogs before we find the answer to that question. I certainly had to! And it's worth the effort.

So, if you find yourself, sadly but with head held high, walking out the door, remember that there are many beautiful men out there who would love being in a loving relationship with you. Your task now is to learn how to recognize them. Onward!

Barbara asks:

How do I let go of someone who hurt me very badly? We went together for three years and then were on and off for about one year. It's been six months since the final breakup and I still find myself angry, empty and lost without him. Help!

Susan answers:

Healing the hurts after a breakup takes time. Not to worry. You will get to the other side! You may want to look at *Losing a Love . . . Finding a Life,* which is actually my own "diary" of breaking up with my first husband and getting to the other side.

You say you are angry. The anger has got to go. It's devastating to your health and future relationships. Remember that your guy did the very best he could at the time . . . and so did you.

Anger often comes from the victim mentality. You have to stop playing the role of "poor me" and create a new model for yourself . . . that of a loving, creative, powerful, and abundant adult. With this new model, you have less to be angry about and more to celebrate!

You also say you feel empty and lost. You certainly would be wise to "find a life" before trying again to share a life. Commit to giving your time, energy and love to family, friends, career and community. Trust me when I tell you that you are a meaningful part of the world around you and when you start giving of yourself you will find the sense of joy you are really looking for. Your goal is to feel whole . . . even without a relationship.

As you begin increasing the richness of your life, your

neediness will disappear and the possibility of a wonderful relationship will increase dramatically. Always remember that LIFE IS HUGE! Look around and embrace it all.

You have an opportunity to use this experience to figure out what you need to work on within yourself to create a healthier relationship in the future. It's like sculpting . . . just keep cutting away what doesn't look like love. I must admit that between my marriages I had a lot of sculpting to do. But I FINALLY got it right . . . and I had a lot of fun along the way!

Jess asks:
I have a real problem with my Mother. She continually criticizes me in my choice of boyfriend, clothes, spending habits, etc. Nothing I do seems to be right for her. I'm single at the moment, but even if I did find a boyfriend I would rather keep him secret than have her criticize his dress or manners. I know my Mother is a bit "moany" in her nature, but I do love her. I would just like her to let me make my own choices and rejoice in those choices. Can you give me any help with improving my relationship with her?

Susan answers:
Jess, I identify with your problem since I had a Mother just like yours. It caused a lot of friction between us until I realized one day that it wasn't what my Mother said that was the problem, *it was how I reacted to what she said.* I then set about changing my reactions to her. Ultimately, I learned how to thank her for her opinions, give her a big kiss, tell her I love her, and go on to do whatever I felt was right for me.

Don't expect her to "rejoice in your choices". She probably isn't going to. For whatever reason, that's not who she is. Just appreciate all she has done to raise the beautiful person you have become.

When we have these "Mother expectations", it means that we haven't fully grown up and we still need approval from our parents. You don't need this approval any more. You are an adult. This is a perfect opportunity for you to work on letting go of this need for approval; if you don't let go of it with your Mother, you will take this need with you to all your future relationships. Not good!

Be proud of who you are, be thankful for your Mother, give her a kiss for the both of us (since my Mother is no longer alive), and go on to live the best kind of life you can ever live.

Julia asks:

I have lived with my partner for two of the three-and-a-half years we've been together, and we have a wonderful relationship. However, we have been arguing a lot recently over the fact that he remains legally married—to someone else. He separated from his wife nearly five years ago, and has no emotional ties to her. Nor are there are any outstanding arrangements to be made regarding their children. I'd like to get married, but have not raised the subject with him. I have, however, nagged him to get divorced. I know he loves me, but he hates being told what to do, and takes ages to make decisions . . . and remains married to someone else. What should I do?

Susan Answers:

Julia, I believe your partner is frightened, not stubborn. He may not even realize it, but he is afraid to "close the door" to the past. Tradition, guilt, money and all manner of things enter the picture. But you have to consider your own life.

I suggest you tell him you love him very much but that he has a choice—to close the door to the past or close the door to a future with you. Then stop the nagging and, in your own mind, create a time limit as to how long you will remain in the relationship. Use that time to gently pull away emotionally by focusing your attention elsewhere, such as spending time with friends and participating in some volunteer activities.

As you become stronger, less needy, and therefore less "naggy", he will realize that it's just a matter of time when he will lose you. Either he will decide to get the divorce or he may still be too frightened to close the door to the past. In any case, you will be fine.

If he gets his divorce, you get your man. (Whether he will then be ready for marriage is another story . . . but you can deal with that when you come to it.) If he doesn't get a divorce, you get the freedom to find a less complicated relationship. Either way, you're a winner!

Angela asks:
I am a 26-year-old woman and I share an apartment with my younger sister. We get on well most of the time, but the trouble is, she hates my boyfriend and whenever he comes round, we end up arguing. Now she's said she doesn't want him coming to the apartment anymore—but I pay half the rent so I don't think she's being fair. How can I resolve this situation without falling out with my sister *or* my boyfriend?

Susan answers:

Angela, you didn't mention why your sister objects to your boyfriend. It may have something to do with his behavior, or sisterly jealousy, or a lack of privacy, or something else entirely.

But whatever it is, your next step seems pretty clear to me: If you want to keep seeing your boyfriend AND you want to remain friends with your sister, you need to find another place to live, preferably alone or, if finances don't permit, with a new room mate. Understand that this truly isn't a case of choosing your boyfriend over your sister; it's about becoming your own person.

It is important to explain to your sister in a very loving way that you need the freedom to live life the way you see fit . . . and that you understand that she needs this freedom as well. There is no right or wrong, or fair or unfair here. It's just two sisters with different needs.

Explain that it is BECAUSE you love her and want to remain friends that it is better to live in separate spaces. In the beginning, she may be very angry, but as time goes by and as you keep sending her loving energy, I trust she will understand.

Don't be dismayed if your present boyfriend isn't the one you ultimately end up with, but you owe it to yourself to see the relationship through to the finish . . . whether that's next month or "till death us do part."

So find another apartment, cut the cord to any dependency you and your sister may have on each other, and live life as a great adventure! Drop the guilt, trusting that you will BOTH learn and grow from this valuable experience.

"Genuinely concerned" asks:
I've been happily married for five years and for some reason I have yet to understand, I have a tendency to get "tipsy" at pubs with my friends and end up kissing total strangers. I've never had an affair and never wanted to, but feel guilty about this absurd behavior. It seems perfectly innocent at the time and I justify it by telling myself that it has no bearing on my marriage or my love for my husband. If it's so innocent, why do I feel like this? If not, why do I keep doing it?

Susan answers:
Genuinely concerned, I'm glad you are genuinely concerned! That's the first step toward making some changes. You ask, "Why do I feel guilty?" Let me ask you this: How would you feel if your husband got 'tipsy' at pubs with his friends and ended up kissing total strangers? I don't think you'd feel good. While your kisses may seem innocent, they certainly aren't respectful to your husband.

You then ask, "Why do I do it?" You do it because you and alcohol don't mix very well. In fact, alcohol has become your enemy. It is threatening your marriage . . . and your safety. Who knows how these strangers will interpret your "innocent" kiss and what they may do as a follow-up?

So, for the love of yourself and for the love of your husband, stop drinking so much or stop drinking altogether. If you can't help yourself, enlist the help of your friends to slow you down. If they won't help you, find some new friends.

In the end, you may need some help from one of the many alcohol dependency programs available today. You may not think you have a problem with alcohol, but if neither you nor your friends can stop you from becoming "tipsy" and acting in an out-of-control manner, think again!

Please, save your dignity, and save all those wonderful kisses for your husband. You both deserve this healthy solution.

Let me assure you that there is absolutely no reason for you to feel guilty. You have noticed that you have a problem and you are now going to take steps to solve it. That's what life is all about . . . learning and growing. And once you handle this situation, you will be a much wiser, happier and loving person.

Marianne asks:

I have a very demanding job . . . and so does my mate. As a result, we hardly see each other. How do you keep a relationship together when the world wants to separate you?

Susan answers:

This is a big challenge in today's busy world. It takes a great deal of creativity in order to keep love alive these days. So you have to become very creative! Here are a few suggestions to get you started.

First, both of you need to ask yourselves: "Do I really have to work so hard or is it that I simply can't say 'NO' to extra tasks I am given?" If it is the latter, FEEL THE FEAR AND SAY NO ANYWAY! If your constant over-working is a requirement of the job, you may want to think about changing jobs.

Second, become a romantic. There are many ways to connect even when we are apart from those we love. For example, you can use e-mails to "loving" advantage. Every day . . . yes, every day . . . my husband and I send each other romantic e-mails expressing our love and thanks. My heart sings every time I receive one. (And he is working in the next room!) Find creative ways to let your sweetheart know he is in your heart even when you are apart.

Third, save the weekends for each other. Obviously, we sometimes have to "catch up" with other things on the weekend, but so many couples go off in separate directions—even when they have the opportunity to be together. Every now and then, create special weekends just for the two of you. If you want to make a relationship work, it has to be a top priority in your life.

Fourth, when you are together, focus on the good stuff. Don't waste your time blaming, arguing or lamenting. Focus on what's wonderful. Keep the romance high with candlelit baths, long walks, intimate talks, and lots of cuddling. Here's your goal: Make your time together so wonderful that, by hook or by crook, you will "magically" find ways to create more and more time to be together.

© 2001 Susan Jeffers, Ph.D.

31.

A Tribute to a Hero

I RECEIVED SOME VERY SAD NEWS the other day. One of my heroes has died. Her name was Sally Lefkowitz. I refer to Sally as a hero because even though she encountered great physical and emotional difficulties throughout her life, she rejected the "victim mentality" and never stopped contributing to this world in her own unique and wonderful way. A great model for us all!

I included Sally in a chapter in *Embracing Uncertainty* entitled "Collecting Heroes". At the time I wrote about her, she was still an active and participating member of the New York community. And I described her impact on me as follows . . .

I met Sally during the time I was Executive Director of The Floating Hospital where, lucky for me, she became a Board Member. In addition to her role as wife and mother, she was actively involved in contributing her time, money and efforts to charities that helped the poor and disabled. Then one day, she had a stroke that put her permanently in a wheelchair.

I'll never forget one particular evening shortly after Sally's stroke occurred. The Floating Hospital, as its name suggests, was aboard a ship. We were having a big fundraiser that, prior to her stroke, Sally had been very actively involved in organizing. She had invited many people to come to the event with the hope that they would get involved in supporting our many activities . . . as she had done. As the staff and I were preparing to welcome everyone aboard for our evening cruise around Manhattan, I felt so sorry that she would not be there to enjoy the fruits of her labors.

Just as this thought was going through my mind, I glanced towards the end of the pier. And there to my surprise and delight was Sally being wheeled down the pier by her husband. I ran to greet her, gave her a big hug and with tears in my eyes thanked her for coming. She spoke with great difficulty (she has thankfully fully recovered her speech), but was able to convey to me that she wanted to welcome aboard the people she had invited to let them know how much The Floating Hospital meant to her.

There she was . . . unable to speak properly, her face partially paralyzed, unable to walk, still shaky and exhausted from her ordeal, but she didn't let us down. She didn't stay for the entire event, but she was there to welcome her guests and set the tone for all of us. By making this supreme effort, she let us know that what we were doing was important. And she let her guests know that what they could do to help us was also important.

Many years have passed and Sally is now in her nineties. She remains in a wheelchair, but she doesn't let that destroy her Spirit. She let's NOTHING destroy her Spirit, even the death of her wonderfully loving husband a few years after her stroke. Throughout her life, she has had almost every ailment that can befall a human being, including cancer, tuberculosis, a stroke, and she is now facing possible blindness, but NOTHING stops her from being a meaningful part of the world.

She still appears at the Board meetings of the various charities she supports. She still helps others in any way she can. She still enjoys the park. She still eats lunch regularly at her favorite restaurant, The Russian Tea Room. And she'll always be a role model and a hero to me. While I frequently tell her so, I want to thank her publicly. So . . .

Thank you, Sally Lefkowitz. I love you.
You truly are a hero to me.

Just before *Embracing Uncertainty* was released, Sally's health badly deteriorated. The last time I visited her in New York, I knew the end was near. I sat by her bedside and read her the above passage, which I told her would soon be spreading around the world in the pages of my new book. Her eyes were closed, and I wasn't sure that she was even hearing me. But, as I read, a big smile appeared on her face and tears flowed from the corners of her eyes. In my heart, I knew she heard . . . and fully took in the meaning of my words. I will always remember that special moment.

With great love and admiration, it's now time for me to say, "Goodbye, Sally . . . you will be missed . . . and you will be remembered for all the love you have given to this world."

© 2003 Susan Jeffers, Ph.D.

32.

Loving the Beat:
The Power of Drums

I HAVE ALWAYS ENJOYED many types of music. But my life changed the day I "discovered" rock music. Of course, many people have been fed by the wonder of rock music throughout their lives, but I discovered it only recently . . . at my age! In the past, I avoided it like the plague as I felt it was much too noisy. I always looked with disdain at those cars stopping next to me at traffic lights with their windows wide open and their rock music blaring. My only thought was, "Have they no consideration of others?"

And then one day it happened. A new television show called The Sopranos was about to debut. It had been given much advance notice in the press, so at the appointed time, Mark and I sat eagerly waiting for it to air. The big moment came. The credits began to roll . . . and I was in love with the show before the credits stopped rolling. Why? The opening theme song was exhilarating! I was all revved up. I felt powerful. I loved that song!

Eagerly I awaited the next episode so that I could hear the opening theme song once again. Each week as the show began, I would sit there with the volume up to the ceiling with my head "nodding" to the beat. Hmm. I was behaving just like those rude dudes that I previously looked at with disdain when I stopped at a traffic light and heard their music blasting. Did they know something I was just discovering?

I mentioned this strange phenomenon to my kids, who each in their own way is involved in the world of music. And when Christmas-time came around, guess what Santa Claus bought me? An album consisting of much of the music played throughout each episode of the Sopranos, including, of course, the amazing theme song. Heaven. Now I could play it any time I wanted . . . almost. I had to go out and buy another copy so I could have one for the house and one for the car. Now I could truly play it any time I wanted.

My car soon became a temple of LOUD music . . . in fact, I played the music so loud, that the car seat vibrated as I drove down the highway. What a high! I could get into my car feeling a bit tired but, in a very short time, I was bouncing with the sounds permeating my little piece of the road. And now when I pulled up next to a car with the music blaring, I no longer felt disdain. The driver and I would turn to look at each other and nod with a smile of recognition and a sense of connection. We both understood the amazing power of the music we were playing.

With the help of my husband and kids, I soon collected additional pieces of rock music that made my spirits soar. At some point, I asked myself what was so special about these particular tracks that made such a difference in my body, mind, and Soul. After all, it wasn't ALL rock music that had this effect on me. Only certain pieces. And then it came to me. The common denominator of all the music I loved was the particular BEAT and the amazing use of the DRUMS! Of course, that was it. THE BEAT OF THE DRUMS TRULY MADE ME HIGH.

So what was the logical next step? To buy myself a set of drums and take drumming lessons. What else? As it transpired, I didn't even have to buy them. My friend, Henry, had a drum set just taking up room in his basement. He said I could have them. Fantastic! And my kids bought me a fine new set of cymbals to go with the drum set and I was ready! I consulted with our friend, Stewart Copeland, who began his phenomenal career as the drummer for The Police. If anyone could guide me, it was him! He told me to find a teacher and just say I wanted to learn the "heavy back beat" (whatever that meant). But Stewart understood!

I found a local music store that taught the drums along with many other instruments. And once a week, I appeared for my lesson. My teacher, Todd, was very patient with me. And I had a great time. I might add that all the other students were under the age of ten, which is why all the classes began after school hours. I would join all the kids waiting for their teachers with their trumpets, or flutes, or violins or whatever. They looked at me kind of strangely as I waited for Todd with my drum sticks; I could have been their grandmother! But I didn't care. I loved it!

And each day I went down to the basement of our house to practice. I drummed and drummed and drummed . . . always with one of my favorite pieces of music playing loudly by my side. Mark said it was as though there were two construction crews hammering away, but he got a lot of joy from the joy I was getting from it all. That's true love! And thankfully, none of the neighbors heard the ruckus. I'm a good neighbor . . . I checked. So all was well.

My rhapsody in the basement went on for about a year. I was having a great time! But, alas, my drumming days would soon come to an end. One day Mark and I decided it was time to sell our house. The housing market was booming and we definitely wanted to down-size. It took a few months, but it finally happened. We found a buyer . . . and had to vacate the house.

We chose to live in a high-rise apartment house where we would have been very unpopular with the neighbors if I were to continue pounding on the drums. (Any apartment dwellers out there know exactly what I am talking about.) And with a bit of sadness, I took my drum set back to Henry. I still cherish my beautiful cymbals that sit there to remind me of how great the drumming felt . . . and how great my kids are. I was told I could continue with a simulated drum set that is on the market, but it wouldn't be the same thing. Better to just move on to other things.

Yes, the drums are gone, but the experience will be with me forever. In fact, I now have an even greater appreciation of the drums that I wouldn't have had without my personal hands-on experience. And my car has become my musical haven.

You might be curious to know which 10 songs are blaring in my car at the present time. So as not to disappoint you . . . here they are . . .

A3—The Sopranos theme song: *Woke Up This Morning* (*Chosen One* Mix)

Michael Wandmacher—*Take a Piece of Me*

Led Zeppelin—*Kashmir*

Phil Collins—*Both Sides of the Story*

M People—*Search for the Hero*

Bon Jovi—*It's My Life*

The Verve—*Bitter Sweet Symphony*

Keith Richards—*Make No Mistake*

The Pretenders—*Space Invader*

I thank and acknowledge the above for giving me and so many others so much joy.

You might think my story ends here, but it doesn't. Not long ago, Mark and I were taking a walk on the beach near our new apartment house on a beautiful Sunday afternoon. As we walked, we began to hear the vibrating sounds of drumming. Music to my ears! Excited and curious, we followed the sounds and in the distance saw a large "drumming circle" consisting of at least 100 drums. As we got closer, we were astounded by the sounds and sights: Men and women ages 18 to 80, every color of skin, and every kind of drum imaginable—African, rock, bongo, and so on—all in a large circle drumming to the same African beat. It was mesmerizing. We sat down in the midst of the drums so that we were able to FEEL the vibrations throughout our bodies. In a few moments we were practically in a meditative state—totally becoming a part of the sounds and scene.

At one point in time the beat suddenly changed . . . and the entire drum circle effortlessly went with it. It was as though there was a Soul-connection in the Circle . . . a vibration . . . that was transmitted to every one of the drummers at the same time. Certainly not a word was spoken, no direction was given, and many of the drummers had their eyes closed and were lost in the beat, but somehow they became part of the flowing energy and were carried along with it. Understand that these were not all expert drummers. A few actually had kitchen pots that defined their drums . . . but they certainly knew when to change their beat.

What occurred to me at that moment, was that the beat of the drums was a stunning vehicle of connection. It didn't matter the age, the color of the skin, the kind of drum, the experience of the drummer. It was the beat that united everyone. Powerful. Mark commented that the drums were a wonderful vehicle for letting out aggression. That is probably true. And they are also a wonderful vehicle for opening the heart. Love certainly was in the air . . . and on the faces of the drummers.

The drum circle is part of the beach scene every Sunday afternoon. And it has become part of our weekend happiness. We are either standing up dancing in the sand or we just sitting there taking in the ecstasy of the moment. Yesterday was particularly special. We were there from about 4:00 to 6:00 p.m. Magic was in the air as we watched the sailboats on the water, the sun going down, a flock of birds flying in perfect formation, the planes in the distance taking off from Los Angeles airport . . . and the drummers pounding out their marvelous sounds. And there were the spectators such as Mark and me, sitting in the miracle of it all. I turned to Mark and said, "Can you imagine a more perfect moment?" We agreed it truly was the best of all possible worlds.

We have finally decided to buy our own little easy-to-carry African drums, so that we too can become part of the drumming circle . . . part of the Circle of love. So the happy ending to this story is that once again, I will be able to say, "I am a drummer." Heaven!

33.

Getting Out of Yourself
to Find Yourself

THERE ARE TIMES ON OUR JOURNEY through the huge-ness of life that we feel lost, unloved, helpless and defeated. What do we do when we find ourselves in such an unhappy state? Some of us escape into the land of danger and defeat. We "get out of ourselves" by drinking too much, or taking drugs, or feeling sorry for ourselves, or complaining, or whatever else that stops us from doing what is truly necessary . . . and that is taking responsibility for our own experience of life. And we look out at the world with envy imagining that everyone else out there has been given a more fulfilling and enjoyable life than we have. Not good!

There are many healthier and happier alternatives. One of these alternatives, which is simple but HUGE in its force, is to "get out of ourselves" by getting involved in the lives of others who are less fortunate. What does that look like? We help feed and clothe the poor; we help build houses for those who have no homes; we visit the homes for the aged; we read to children in hospitals . . . and all manner of such beautiful things.

When I was the Executive Director of The Floating Hospital, which provided all sorts of health, educational and recreational activities for the poor in New York City, I relied on the help, not only of a paid staff, but a large number of volunteers. These beautiful beings provided money, services, time, energy, love, and caring to help those less fortunate than themselves.

Understand that not all of these volunteers were the moneyed of the community. I met "poor helping poor", people giving to their community in ways that touched the Soul. They taught me so much about what makes life worth living. And what truly does make life worth living is not only *finding* love, caring and all good things for one's self. No, it's also about *giving* love, caring and all good things to others.

It's not that *getting* isn't wonderful . . . it is. And learning how to take with gratitude is a sign of an open heart and brings us much joy. But giving has its own special rewards. It is the pathway to finding and increasing our feelings of self-confidence and worth. And in the end, *it is just these feeling that we are all yearning for during those times when our lives seem so empty and unhappy.*

At The Floating Hospital, I saw firemen, policemen, society women, doctors, college students and so many other segments of society all showing up to distribute lunches, play with the children, wash the dishes, sing songs, create new programs, do office work, raise money and whatever else was needed. And in so doing, they discovered the incredible feeling of well-being inherent in the act of giving. How lucky they were and how lucky were those they served!

One of the people who often volunteered was my daughter, Leslie. She began learning at the age of ten what it meant to give of herself. She stuffed envelopes, washed dishes and served coffee with the best of them. And she carried this learning into adulthood. One of her ways of getting out of herself today is to volunteer for Habitat for Humanity, a wonderful organization that builds houses for people who can't afford to do it themselves. I have photographs of her happily hammering nails on the roof of a house-in-progress. She talks about her feeling of joy and healthy pride when the keys to that finally-completed house are handed over to a family who never before had a decent place in which to live. In many other ways, Leslie has never stopped her practice of getting out of herself to find more of herself.

Ely, a friend of mine who had a stroke, was able to feel blessed and abundant every time he volunteered, wheelchair and all, to help cook in a restaurant that served free meals to the homeless. He knew he counted and had much to give to the community, despite his stroke. And it was his acts of giving that always made his spirits soar. As a general rule, to know that we count is one of the greatest boosts to our morale that we can ever experience. By the way, some of us volunteer at Holiday time, which is wonderful. But those who get the most out of volunteering are those who make it a regular part of their lives . . . not just a Holiday special.

You might be wondering why volunteering makes you feel so good about yourself? As I see it, volunteering takes you out of your Lower Self, the negative part of who you are, and elevates you to your Higher Self . . . the best of who you are . . . the part of you that is loving, powerful and abundant. You can understand why, when you find your way from the Lower Self to the Higher Self, your experience of life is transformed in a magnificent way.

So here is what I suggest: Any time you feel yourself in a depressed and unhappy state, immediately get up and get out to help the world in any way you can. And as you make helping others a part of your everyday life, any feelings of depression and unhappiness will appear less and less and less . . . and feelings of joy, gratitude and all good things will appear more and more and more. It works every time.

See, I told you the answer was simple, but HUGE in its force.

© 2000 Susan Jeffers, Ph.D.

34.

Finding Peace of Mind in a Very Uncertain World

There is great adventure in the unknown that propels us to discover powerful parts of ourselves that we didn't know were there.

AS I WRITE THIS ARTICLE, my eyes focus on the cover of our leading news magazines. They tell us that ANXIETY is the number one issue at the moment. And it is true. We are an anxious world.

There is no question that uncertainty seems to have increased dramatically in the last few years. We worry about terrorism. We worry about the economy. We worry about the dangers confronting our children. We worry about deadly new illnesses that pop up from time to time. And on and on and on.

This anxiety is understandable, given the state of the world at the present time, but there is no question in my mind that, given the right tools . . .

—all of us can rise above any situation that life hands us . . .

—all of us can live a fulfilling life in the middle of the turmoil . . .

—all of us can find a sense of peace and purpose.

With this in mind, I wrote *Embracing Uncertainty* to give you "the right tools" to help you see the world in a more life-affirming and powerful way. To get you started on the path toward peace of mind, let me give you a few tools to get you started:

"UN-SET" YOUR HEART. Un-setting your heart means letting go of your picture of how you want it all to be. It means letting go of trying to control things over which you have no control. Trust me when I tell you that one of the prime causes of our suffering is our wanting things to be different than they are. Yes, we all want a peaceful world instead of a world filled with weapons of mass destruction. Yes, we all want health instead of illness. Yes, we all want healthy, happy children instead of children who break our hearts. But sometimes life doesn't hand us what we want. And when we un-set our hearts to our needing it all to be a certain way, we can breathe a sigh of relief and open the door to a much more powerful way of living. Read on.

CREATE A "WONDERING" LIFE INSTEAD OF A "HOPING" LIFE. It helps us un-set our hearts when we substitute the words "I hope" with the words "I wonder". Let me demonstrate. Instead of "I hope we don't go to war", make it "I wonder if we'll go to war." Instead of "I hope the stock market goes up", make it "I wonder if the stock market will go up." Instead of "I hope I keep my job", make it "I wonder if I'll keep my job." Notice the relief in this simple shift. Instead of placing yourself in the middle of the drama with your hopes, wishes, wants and desires, you have placed yourself in the role of observer of how it will all turn out . . . as if you were watching a good movie unfold. "How interesting. I wonder what comes next." And you do this with the understanding that no matter how it all turns out, you will learn and grow from it all.

CHOOSE THE PATH OF TRUST. What do I mean by "choosing the path of trust?" When you fully understand that you have little control in the external world, you then have two choices: you can choose to see yourself as a "poor-me" victim at the mercy of circumstances . . . or you can choose to develop the trust that, no matter what happens in your life or in the world, you will have the inner strength to create something good from it all. Hopefully you will choose the latter.

INCREASE YOUR INNER SENSE OF POWER. One way to help you develop trust in yourself is to cut off the negativity in the mind by saying to yourself over and over again, "Whatever happens in my life, I'll handle it!" Those of you who know my work know that it is one of my favorite affirmations. I suggest you emblazon this powerful thought in your mind. If you say it often enough, you will ultimately believe it! And if you really believe that you can handle anything that happens in your life and in the world, what could you possibly have to fear? Nothing!

So when the "what-if's" are driving you mad, simply cut them off by saying over and over again, "Whatever happens, I'll handle it!" You'll feel a sense of confidence wash over you. "What if I lose my job? I'll handle it." "What if my children have difficult times? I'll handle it." "What if I get ill? "I'll handle it."

"Whatever happens in my life, I'll handle it!"

Powerful, indeed!

COLLECT "HEROES" WHO HAVE LEARNED TO HANDLE IT ALL. Heroes to me are people who have created much good in this world as a result of horrible experiences in their lives. A few heroes come to mind: Christopher Reeve, who created so much good as a result of his paralyzing accident; Viktor Frankl, who created so much good out of his experience in a concentration camp; Ram Dass, who created so much good as a result of his debilitating stroke; Marc Klaas, who created so much good after the murder of his daughter. And I could go on and on and on. As you collect heroes, you understand this important thought,

"If they can learn and grow from their experiences, I certainly can learn and grow from mine!"

As you collect your heroes . . . your models . . . you are filled with a sense of trust and your worry about the future gets smaller and smaller.

FOCUS ON THE LEARNING THAT CAN COME FROM ANY SITUATION IN YOUR LIFE. Yes, you can learn and find strength from ANYTHING that happens to you, just as the above heroes have done. I certainly learned from and found strength as a result of my own experiences with cancer and my divorce from my first husband. If you see ALL situations in life as a way of learning and growing, it helps you let go of your need for things to be a certain way . . .

War. . . . . a way of learning
Peace. . . . . a way of learning
Illness . . . . a way of learning
Health. . . . . . . a way of learning
Poverty . . . . . . a way of learning
Wealth . . . . . . a way of learning
Depression . . . a way of learning
Joy . . . . a way of learning

So despite what is happening in your life and in the world, constantly remind yourself "I CAN LEARN FROM THIS." When you can see the opportunities inherent in ALL situations . . . good or bad . . . it truly helps you embrace all the uncertainty in your life.

EMBRACE THE THOUGHT "IT'S ALL HAPPEN-ING PERFECTLY." This is another affirmation I use over and over again. And it truly helps me let go of my needing things to be a certain way. "Susan, how can things be happening perfectly when there is possibility of terrorism, illness, poverty and violence?". My answer to that is we cannot know the Grand Design, the great mystery of it all, and as we say "It's all happening perfectly", we begin looking for the "good" in any situation that life hands us. And when we look for the good, WE ALWAYS FIND IT. Yes, so much good can come from so much that is bad. In that, it truly is happening perfectly.

So when things seem very difficult in your life or in the world, just keep repeating this reassuring statement over and over again until it becomes an automatic part of your thinking. I have this affirmation sitting on my desk and whenever things seem to be going badly, I look at these reassuring words and repeat them over and over again.

It's all happening perfectly!
It's all happening perfectly!
It's all happening perfectly!

This phrase always helps me to have trust, not only in myself, but also "the Grand Design."

FOCUS ON THE RICHES. I have learned from my heroes that, no matter how horrible life may seem on the outside, it is so important to focus on the beauty. As we go about our daily lives, we take so many wonderful things for granted. It's now time to notice. Strangely, this is hard to do, especially when we have our eyes focused on the bad. It sounds ridiculous, but we actually have to train ourselves to notice all the beauty in our lives! And train ourselves, we must . . . because focusing on the blessings is an absolute necessity for diffusing our fears about the future.

A suggestion: As you go about your day, stop for a moment and notice when something wonderful happens. Then say to yourself while still in the glory of the moment, "I HAVE HAD THIS." This is the acknowledgement that "No matter what happens tomorrow, I have had this today." Notice the little things, for it is in the noticing of the little things that you truly get the feeling of a life well-lived . . . that wonderful hot shower, that kiss from a loved one, the fact that your car started, that great dinner you are eating, the warm rays of the sun, a candy bar, a wonderful television show . . . and on and on and on.

You can write your I HAVE HAD THIS moments on little slips of paper and at the end of the day put them into your I HAVE HAD THIS jar—which is simply a clear glass jar with a sticker that says I HAVE HAD THIS. In a very short time, you will see your riches add up to a life well-lived. In fact, you will have to get a bigger jar! When that happens, you truly begin to lose the sense that life is passing you by. Instead, you are walking right along with life and gathering all that it has to offer. You are not missing a thing. It stands to reason that you worry less and less about the future as you appreciate life to its fullest NOW!

GET INVOLVED. Positive action has an amazing effect on our psyche. As we take action, we begin to feel more powerful and our fear about the future decreases considerably. Keep repeating to yourself . . .

"My life has meaning and I will do whatever I can to make this a better world."

Then: 1) ask yourself, "What am I asked to do?", 2) make a list of what comes to mind, and 3) begin taking action. When you remember that your life has meaning, it makes it so much easier to push through the fear and live a life that matters. And your self-esteem grows and grows. Just as importantly, you will have found the secret of creating a joyous and fulfilling life.

The above offers you a great way to begin. You can learn much more about these tools and many others in

Embracing Uncertainty. As you make these tools a part of your daily life . . .

—you experience a whole new sense of purpose emerging from within . . .
—you begin to trust that you are more powerful than you could ever have imagined . . .
—and, while enjoying the present, you look forward to the future with an attitude of great possibility— for yourself and for your world.

I think you'll agree that it doesn't get any better than that!

© 2003 Susan Jeffers, Ph.D.

35.

The Land of Tears

TRAFFIC WAS VERY HEAVY and as I sat looking out the window of the bus, I noticed a group of schoolchildren walking in twos, heading for the park. It was a warm sunny day in May, and the children's giggles and chatter that I heard through the open window put a smile on my face. Each child carried a lunch bag filled with little treasures that some caring person had placed there earlier that morning. My mind got lost in thinking back to those special days when I was a child.

My reverie was suddenly shattered when one little boy's lunch bag burst open, spilling all his treasures on the ground. As I watched his anguished gaze fixated on the ruined contents of his bag, I had to turn away. Somewhere deep within me, it hurt too much, and the tears started rolling down my cheeks.

I was surprised at the well of emotion this little incident had released in me. My reaction seemed totally inappropriate to the scene that had occurred. What was going on within me? From where did my deep sadness come?

I then realized that this was not the first time I had felt this puzzling depth of emotion over some relatively innocuous scene that I had witnessed. This was not the first time that some situation outside myself had touched that place within that I have come to call the Land of Tears.

I knew that the deep sadness that I felt had nothing to do with what was happening in my life at the time. In fact, my life was rich with meaningful work and the love of my family and caring friends. No, the sadness was not about my personal story, but something much bigger, wider and deeper than that. Another perplexing part of the puzzle was that, not only did sad things touch the Land of Tears, happy things did as well. Just watching a family reunited at the airport left me sobbing. What was that all about?

The answer was not something I came to easily. Through much soul-searching, I eventually found the answers to my questions. I came to realize that my tears reflected something I had tried very hard to deny . . . the Universal hardship that we all experience by virtue of the fact that we are human beings. Life is tough! It hurts a lot! By definition, being truly alive implies a lot of pain.

Who has not at times felt rejected, unloved, helpless, lonely, not quite good enough? Who has not cried at the unfairness of so many happenings in their lives? Who has not inwardly prayed that things like death and cancer and nuclear war won't happen to them and theirs? Who has not had to come to terms with the fact that there are times we have to say good-bye to those we love most? Life is about facing all this and so much more.

But why the tears in the face of great joy? This was not too difficult to figure out. Isn't it all part of the same thing? Isn't joy about reaching the other side of struggle?

Didn't that family reunited at the airport first have to go through the pain of separation, time of loneliness, and fear of loss before the joy of reunion? Their tears and hugs suggested they did. Whether it's the sorrow of good-bye or the joy of hello, it's all part of the same package. It all signifies the human condition.

The last and most important part of the puzzle was, "Why did I have to turn away?" This was the tough one. I finally realized it was because I couldn't look life squarely in the face. For years, I tried very hard to avoid the Land of Tears. I needed to believe that life was always great and we should always be happy. To perpetuate this delusion, I became a pseudo-positive thinker, one who was in constant denial about the pain of living. I was avoiding an essential element in the art of genuine positive thinking. I was avoiding the Land of Tears.

I became such a pseudo-positive thinker that I became detached, disconnected from my own pain and disconnected from other people's pain as well. In fact, I dismissed their despair as weakness. They were touching feelings I was desperately trying to disinherit. Hence, I couldn't feel connection and empathy, only disdain.

But trying to uphold the fantasy that this is the best of all possible worlds is a difficult thing to do in the face of overwhelming evidence to the contrary. Just reading the daily newspaper should cause the slightest bit of doubt. Yet I kept trying to convince myself that all was well. It was like the proverbial finger in the dike, trying to hold back the realities of life. It would leak every once in a while . . . such as when I faced with the little boy and his shattered lunch bag.

One day the dike cracked open, and I could no longer hold back the flood of pain. I realized that all the hunger, war, greed, illness, unfairness, pain and horror in the world were real. It was not a figment of anyone's imagination, or a result of negative thinking. The despair poured through me. What a blow to a well-defended personality! It took a while to absorb the shock of my despair and restructure my life in a more genuine and life-affirming way. But it was well worth the effort.

Having made the Land of Tears an integral part of my life so many years ago has had enormous benefits. In the first place, I've joined the human race. When I watch the struggle of others, I can now connect with my own struggle, and we are no longer strangers. I don't have to turn away. I can embrace them and their pain, and let them know they are not alone. I'm a lot kinder and more patient, and that makes me feel good.

I've learned to judge others a lot less harshly, remembering that deep within them exists their own Land of Tears, no matter how they may appear on the outside. What they do and say is just their way of handling hurt. I actually feel younger then I did way back then. I have much more energy. I feel lighter, freer, more able to dance with life. What a merciful relief not to have to hold back that raging river of emotion any longer!

Now, when the deep sadness comes over me, I can let it be there like a warm blanket. I don't have to push it away. It feels so good to just let the tears flow freely. When I let the tears wash over me, I feel cleansed and healed. And when the river of tears is empty, I am able to help the world instead of turning away. And I am freer to enjoy the delights the world has to offer, without a layer of sadness dampening my joy.

Paradoxically, my letting in the pain of being human has allowed me to embrace the joy of being human. The exquisite moments expand and expand . . . the moments I am infused with energy and aliveness, the moments I feel connected as part of the human family, the moments I let go of the struggle and feel myself dancing with life. All the pain in the world cannot deny the existence of these exquisite moments.

(To learn more about the beauty of the *Land of Tears* and how to use it effectively in your own life, go to *End the Struggle and Dance with Life*.)

36.

Bratty Kids! Squabbling Kids!

THERE ARE TIMES when we are appalled by the bratty behavior of our own children. Immediately, we ask ourselves, "Where did we go wrong?" And we are confused as to what are the appropriate steps to turn our children's ugly behavior into angel behavior.

First, relax and stop feeling guilty. You need to realize that all children display bratty behavior at times. It is part of the process of growing up. They come into this world as very needy individuals and needy people will do almost *anything* to get their way . . . much to the dismay of everyone around them!

Second, learn as much as you can about children's behavior, of course. Read books, articles, and reach out to friends and/or professionals. You might get some good ideas. But in the end, (and this is the important part), take what works for you and let the rest go. Excluding physical or verbal abuse, you need to do what FEELS right for who you are as a parent. The experts who tell you how to raise your children really don't know what is right for you or your child. In the end, we need to learn how to trust ourselves.

Third, we do our best and then, as hard as it seems, we must let go of the outcome. How our children ultimately turn out is a very "chancy" thing. So many factors enter into what I call the child's Circle of Being that we really don't know who or what is having the most influence on how they ultimately turn out. They are affected by their parents, of course, but also their genes, their schools, their friends, and a whole host of other things that we can't even begin to imagine. I repeat: We do our very best according to what we believe to be the very best, and then we let go of the outcome.

I do find it unfair that parents are constantly blamed for the behavior of their children. Yes, of course, some negligent parents exist, but most parents do their very best to be there for their children . . . whether they are working parents or stay-at-home parents. Yet, when a child misbehaves there is the immediate judgment that it must be the parent's fault. Not necessarily so. It is probably just a child in the process of growing up. There is very little to stop the obnoxious periods of behavior that so many children go through. The good news is that most of them turn out very well, indeed.

I've been asked, "Okay, I appreciate what you say, but what do I do when my little one is misbehaving in public?" My answer is to remove them, where possible, from the scene. Let me give you an example. You are dining with your child at a lovely restaurant and your child starts screaming. You can't help but notice that angry stares are coming your way! (One of the people staring angrily would be me!) Here is where you do have some control. You immediately remove the child until the screaming stops and then return with a sense of dignity. You have spared other people the screaming of your child.

Screaming children can certainly ruin a wonderful meal . . . for all of us. The glares will turn to looks of appreciation when you come back into the room. While you can expect your children to behave "brattily" at times, and that is usually not your fault, you would be kind to take the responsibility to see that it doesn't affect the innocent people around you.

A word about "squabbling kids": It's bad enough having a bratty kid, but what do you do with squabbling kids? Two brats instead of one! While squabbling kids are difficult to be around, I don't believe that we are doing a bad job as parents just because our children are squabbling. It's a fact: most siblings fight with each other . . . often. It just seems to be part of the process of their growing up. They seem to derive great satisfaction from the attention their squabbling brings them . . . and for some children, no amount of attention is enough. (Perhaps those who choose to have only one child know exactly what they are doing!)

I don't believe that there is any set way of handling sibling spats. We, as parents, need to experiment and see what works best for ourselves and for our children. And, most importantly, we need to lighten up about it all. Just between us, I came up with a very winning way to stop my kids when they were squabbling. I would start singing a song . . . LOUDLY. Trust me when I tell you they would stop fighting immediately . . . just to shut me up! My words of admonishment rarely made a difference, but my singing loudly truly did! So experiment and find what works for you. And console yourself with the fact that one day they will be all grown up and the squabbling will stop

. . . maybe! But at least by then, they will be out of the house and out of earshot. Ah, peace at last."

(To learn more about the experience of raising children, read *I'm Okay . . . You're a Brat*.)

37.

Susan's Rules for a Huge . . . and Joyous . . . Life

I'VE DEVISED 20 RULES for creating a fantastic life for my time on this earth . . . rules that I've learned over the years. When I follow them, my life is beyond wonderful. Of course, once in a while, I don't follow them, and my life is definitely less than wonderful! And sooner or later, I'm back to following the rules once again . . . and everything improves.

I would like to share my special rules with you. I believe that if you choose to follow them, your life will certainly be HUGE . . . filled with love, with joy, with adventure, with all good things. Of course, you can play with them at will and make them your own, but here are the basics . . .

1.
WITH EYES OF GRATITUDE,
NOTICE ALL THE BEAUTY AROUND YOU.

2.
SMILE AS YOU RECOGNIZE
THE MANY BLESSINGS IN YOUR LIFE.

3.

**JOYFULLY SAY "THANK YOU"
TO ALL WHO CONTRIBUTE TO YOUR LIFE.**

4.

**PICK UP THE MIRROR AND ASK,
"HOW CAN I BE MORE HELPFUL HERE?"**

5.

**COMMIT TO PUTTING MORE
LOVE INTO EVERYTHING YOU DO.**

6.

**KNOW THAT YOU COUNT . . .
AND ACT AS IF YOU DO.**

7.

**FEEL JOY IN THE KNOWLEDGE
THAT YOUR LIFE HAS MEANING.**

8.

**TAKE A DEEP BREATH AND CUT THE
CORD TO ANY UNHEALTHY DEPENDENCY.**

9.

**LET GO OF BLAME, STAND TALL
AND TAKE CONTROL OF YOUR
REACTIONS TO ALL LIFE EXPERIENCES.**

10.

**LEARN SOMETHING VALUABLE FROM
ALL LIFE EXPERIENCES . . .
GOOD OR BAD.**

11.
DO YOUR BEST AND
LET GO OF THE OUTCOME.

12.
ACT RESPONSIBLY AND LOVINGLY
TOWARD YOURSELF AND OTHERS.

13.
RISE ABOVE YOUR FEAR AND FOCUS
ON ALL YOU HAVE TO GIVE TO THE
WORLD.

14.
LET GO AND ALLOW THE RIVER
TO CARRY YOU TO NEW ADVENTURES.

15.
BE PATIENT AND TRUST
"IT'S ALL HAPPENING PERFECTLY".

16.
QUIET YOUR MIND AND TRUST THAT
YOUR INNER WISDOM WILL LEAD YOU
TO WHEREVER YOU NEED TO GO.

17.
RELAX KNOWING YOU CAN HANDLE
ALL THAT NEEDS TO BE HANDLED.

18.
REACH OUT AND INVITE OTHERS
INTO YOUR LIFE.

19.
ALWAYS CHOOSE THE PATH
WITH THE HEART.

20.
TOUCH THE WORLD WITH LOVE
WHEREVER YOU GO.

It may seem like a lot of rules but, if you begin focusing on just one of them every day of your life, I do believe your life will get better . . . and better . . . and better . . . and better. Certainly mine has.

© 2003 Susan Jeffers, Ph.D.

38.

Do Know-It-Alls
Really Know It All?

BERTRAND RUSSELL ONCE SAID the trouble with
the world is that the stupid are cocksure and the intelli-
gent are full of doubt. Hmm. Have you noticed how the
number of know-it-alls seems to have increased recently?
While they have always existed and always will (I used to
be one of them!), the advent of 24 hour television has put
them clearly in view. They are there to convince us that
they truly are right! Cocksure, indeed! The two-pronged
question is "Should we listen to them . . . do they really
know-it-all?"

Let's look at it logically. To be a wise person requires
the ability to listen and learn, which know-it-alls can't
seem to do. By definition, know-it-alls have closed the
door to learning and therefore know much less than they
would if they kept their ears and eyes open. In fact, know-
it-alls seem to live in a world of "blind certainty". By
definition, those who live in a world of blind certainty,
can't "see" very far or wide at all.

If you think about it, it is ironic that, by definition,
know-it-alls close the door to knowing. That's not very
smart! They haven't learned from the scientist, Richard

Feynman, that a "satisfactory philosophy of ignorance" is the key to learning. No, they are locked in an "unsatisfactory philosophy of arrogance" where learning is impossible!

Since know-it-alls have always been part of the scene, why do I bring it up now? As I turn on my television set, I realize that so many "pseudo-experts" with an unyielding need to be right are separating people instead of uniting them. And if ever there was a time for people to be united, this is it. So when I see an abundance of certainty-without-knowing plus an unyielding-need-to-be-right, I get a bit concerned.

We live in an era of escalating uncertainty and fear. And too many know-it-alls on both sides of the issues are making the situation worse. Instead of calming and unifying their listeners, their increasing babble is creating a polarized and jittery world. Of course, the relentless needs of television stations increase the amount of expert bickering . . . it makes a good show. But is this healthy for the world?

Little by little, I watch our world being transformed into an energy of arrogance and anger. This is not a good scenario for creating a more loving world. What the world needs right now is not child-like bickering going on between so-called experts who have an unyielding need to be right. Rather, it needs an openness and exchange of ideas.

Of course, some experts are wise enough to realize that this is a MAYBE world. And they act accordingly. But there are many others who put their claims out into the world as absolute truths. Uncontestable. They "know" they are right. I am amazed when I hear two experts arguing on a talk show? One gives one interpretation of the situation and one gives the opposite interpretation of the situation. This one KNOWS someone committed—or didn't commit—a murder before a trial was even held. This one KNOWS we should go to war—or shouldn't go to war—as if they could see the future. We must ask ourselves, "How do they KNOW?" None of us knows for sure what the future holds . . . no matter how much information we have. If they are both "right", then why are they not in total agreement???

What is most "noticeable" about the two arguing experts is the negative energy created by their arrogance and self-righteousness. In its extreme, self-righteousness creates dogmatism, rigidity and intransigence. Hardly the traits of a wise person! We see this in so many religious and political extremists in today's world. When people are dogmatic, they insist that the rest of the world agree with them. And they denigrate those who don't. And that's how wars are started . . . big wars and little ones.

Over the years, I have encountered many "experts" who provide a perfect example of dogmatism. They KNOW everything. For example, when doing research for my book, *I'm Okay . . . You're a Brat*, I was amazed by the "sureness" of many of the child care experts giving advice to parents. "If you don't follow my advice, your children will grow up as terrorists!" Or something just as dire. I call these child-care experts the "guilt-gurus". To the unsuspecting, it sounds as if they really know what they are talking about.

The experts can guess and they can surmise but, if we just take a look around, we notice that a child can have the worst that life can offer and turn out wonderfully; and a child can have the best that life can offer and turn out horribly. Or, in the same family, one child can turn out to be great and the other horrible. Obviously, there are other factors entering into what I have coined the child's "Circle of Being."

And then there are the health claims. Some experts, for example, tell us that absolutely, for sure, we must eat a low-fat, high carbohydrate diet in order to be healthy. Others tell us that absolutely, for sure, we must eat a high fat, high protein diet in order to be healthy.

What does this tell us? It tells us not to trust either one of them! It tells us that we must be suspicious of any expert who claims to know it all . . . who knows what is best for your health, who knows how to raise a healthy child, and so on. He or she is a pseudo-expert. A real expert of the best kind will tell you, "To the best of my knowledge at the present time, this is the information I have. Maybe I'm right; maybe I'm wrong. Only time will tell . . . maybe!"

Given all the above, we have to ask ourselves, what do we do with the knowledge that our "experts" are giving us. I think that first, we have to be wise enough not to believe they really know the answers as they profess. Maybe they're right; maybe they're wrong. (As I discuss in *Embracing Uncertainty*, there is great power in the word MAYBE!) Then, we need to keep our eyes wide open, listen, do our own research, learn, and then make up our own minds . . . with the idea that we will change our minds if new information guides us in that direction.

I recognize that some of you may be troubled by this realization. Many of us want the experts to have all the answers. And it can be frightening to realize that they don't. But as you learn to feel more comfortable in the "not-knowing state of mind", you are much more open to question, to investigate and to discover. And the wiser you become. Ultimately we learn to trust what feels right to us as human beings . . . maybe.

And what about our own know-it-all behavior? We always want to take action to create a better world for ourselves and others, but we act with the understanding that maybe we're right, maybe we're wrong. When we act in this way, we create a way of being with people with an open energy and an eagerness to learn and to share our ideas with others . . . not as if we knew everything, because we clearly don't, but as a seeker looking to work with others to create a healing answer.

As I said, I used to be a know-it-all. I joke that I am now a recovering know-it-all. I used to think I knew everything. More and more, I am coming to realize that I don't know much about anything . . . and neither does anyone else. I find this a wonderful way to approach life. As I let go of my arrogance and my unyielding need to be right, I am able to listen to the views of others. And I have learned a lot. I also have noticed a definite sense of respect emerging from my being for those with differing points of view. And I have learned that to truly affect the opinions of others, the language of love is the most effective way to go. The language of stridency usually doesn't change anyone's mind . . . it only solidifies the opposing point of view.

There is no question that we pay a price for our need to be right. Our win at any cost mentality reduces us from the loving part of who we are to the losing part of who we are. We might win a particular battle, but we have lost our self-respect. In this case, winning doesn't feel good at all. Thankfully, there is a more loving and enriching way to go. As you open your mind there is an automatic opening of your heart. An open heart is only one reward for living our lives with an open mind. There are many more rewards, indeed. Certainly this has been my experience. And I trust it will be yours as well . . . maybe. Hmm.

39.

After the Breakup:
14 Steps to Happiness

MOST OF YOU HAVE, at one time or another, experienced the breakup of a relationship. Some of you may be going through a breakup right now. Not to worry! I know breakups feel awful. They leave a big empty space in your gut . . . and in your heart. It's certainly the height of wisdom at such a time to enter the Land of Tears and cry . . . a lot. After all, we must mourn the end of an era. But, thankfully, it is by definition also the beginning of a new era. And the possibilities are fantastic.

I speak from experience. In fact, many of you have read *Losing a Love, Finding a Life,* which was my own diary after the painful breakup with my first husband. And certainly after my divorce, I had a number of painful breakups with men I dated along the way . . . all of which ultimately taught me much about loving and being loved. Here are a number of steps I took, and you can take as well, to help get it better the next time around and, just as importantly, to help you value the time in-between.

1) Understand that the relationship that has ended was not a failure . . . as long as you learn and grow from it all. Between my marriages I had LOTS of relationships . . . forty-two, but who's counting. (I guess I had a lot of learning and growing to do!) But I FINALLY got it right . . . and I must say I had a lot of fun along the way.

2) Make a commitment to take control of your experience of life and honor who you are. Back your commitment up with some affirmations that you can repeat to yourself throughout each day. Here are a few to get you started:

I am taking action.
I am now taking control of my life.
I am reclaiming my power.
I am powerful and I am loving
I am creating a life filled with love.

3) Create a very rich life so that the absence of a relationship doesn't wipe you out. One suggestion that I give in *Feel the Fear and Do It Anyway* is to draw a nine-boxed grid . . . and label it your "Grid of Life". In each of the nine boxes, write one aspect of life that is important to you, such as family, friends, career, relationship, contribution to community, spiritual growth, alone time and so on. Then commit to participating fully in every area of your own personal Grid of Life . . . and this is important . . . with the knowledge that you count.

Maybe you feel as if you don't really count. If that is true for you, here is a question you can carry with you all the days of your life . . .

"If I were really important here what would I be doing?"

Ask yourself this question for every area of your Grid . . . and then begin "doing it", one step at a time. You might be asking, "Susan, what is the point of this exercise?" As you look at your Grid of Life, you see relationship is an important part of your life . . . but it isn't your whole life. In fact, YOUR LIFE IS HUGE!

4) Plant seeds of self-respect. With every action you take, keep asking yourself, "How can I be stronger and more loving here?" Always remember that strength and love go together. Without loving actions there is no self-respect; without a sense of inner strength, insecurity reigns and, as a result, it is difficult to be a loving person.

5) Find a positive self-help or therapy-led support group. I find the group process to be incredibly valuable. If you feel adventurous, you can create your own self-help group. A look through your address book and a few phone calls can start the ball rolling. Just three or four people meeting regularly to discuss openly troubling aspects of life will help heal the heart. A word of advice: Self-help groups are not therapy. If a group member appears to be embroiled in an emotional problem that is overwhelming, it is

important that he or she is encouraged to seek professional help.[1]

6) Avoid blame. When we blame other people, in this case our ex-lover, for our unhappiness, we give away all our power. We need to take responsibility for our lives. I think it's called growing up. The positive thing to do is to pick up the mirror instead of the magnifying glass, not to blame ourselves, but to empower ourselves. The question isn't, "How could he (or she) be such a beast?", rather it is something like, "How can I react in a way that makes me feel healthy and whole?" Or, "What must I do within myself to create a healthier relationship the next time?" You get the point.

7) Make a list of everything you want in a mate. For example, "I want a man (woman) who is kind, loving, generous, supportive and on and on and on. Then, the surprising next step . . . *Pick up the mirror and ask, "Which of these qualities am I lacking in myself?" . . . and begin to incorporate them in your being.* Like attracts like. I'm always amused at angry and judgmental people wanting loving and supportive people to love. It's not going to happen! A healthy person would be running the other way. And don't forget it's not about looks! Just look around at happy couples. They're not all "tens!" No, it's not about looks. It's about those qualities that are invisible to the eye.

8) Don't do things just to meet a potential mate. Do things because you love doing them. In this way, you need never come home from an evening disappointed

that you didn't meet anyone; rather you come home happy that you had a good time. If you do happen to meet someone doing what you love to do, the likelihood is that your interests will be more aligned.

9) Learn the value of friends. In *Dare to Connect,* I called friendship "the safety net of the heart." Friends are there to listen, to support, to share, and to help heal the hole in the heart. Of course, to make friendship work, it is important that you are there for your friends as well. Learn to listen, to support, to share and to help in any way they need help. Friends truly are important in our lives for so many, many reasons. So treasure them. Be there for them. Hug them a lot.

10) Learn how to be happily alone. Unless you are happy and complete within yourself, you will be a very needy partner in a relationship. And needy people are not loving . . . as you may have already found out. Start by allowing one evening a week where you come home, lock your door, turn off the phone, cell phone, and any other way that people can communicate with you. Then proceed to do things that bring you pleasure . . . take a soothing hot bath, watch a great movie, meditate, appreciate the fact that you can do anything you want to do in the confines of your own space. You can eat when you want, sleep when you want, have the whole bed to yourself.

When I was single, I had my bed piled with all sorts of goodies—snacks, books, clothes—and I would go to sleep at night enjoying the "comfort" of it all. Delicious. Of course, when I married my present husband, Mark, the snacks, books and clothes were removed and replaced by an alternate source of great pleasure—my husband Mark. Delicious. But those alone times were not without satisfaction. It took a while, but ultimately I began to truly enjoy the alone time. You can do the same.

11) Invite people in your life. Create your own universe. Stop yearning to be a part of someone else's. You never have to be on the outside looking in, when you are the one hosting the party. If reaching out to others is a bit frightening, "feel the fear and do it anyway!" Some may not want to be invited in. That's okay. There are so many loving people in this world who would definitely want to be invited in. You have only to keep asking.

12) Look at the expectations you have of a future mate. If you want your mate to fill you up, you are bound to be disappointed. You have to do that all by yourself. We are still very much in the middle of a transitional period in terms of the roles we play in relationship. This creates great confusion. Rigid and often old-fashioned expectations can destroy a potentially good relationship. I have come a long way when it comes to creating a good relationship. And to me, a healthy relationship is so much about walking the walk and talking the talk . . . together . . . as two powerful and loving adults. Magic.

13) Learn how to love the opposite sex. I guarantee that if you are angry and competitive with the opposite sex, there is very little chance of having a good relationship with a member of the opposite sex. It makes

sense, doesn't it? It's hard to be loving to the enemy! Women, no more male-bashing! Men, no more woman-bashing!

14) As always, have patience with yourself. Take it step-by-step. And with each step you will learn that love . . . and life . . . get better and better and better.

© 2000 Susan Jeffers, Ph.D.

40.

Watching the News
Without Getting Upset

WE LIVE IN A "BAD NEWS WORLD." No doubt
about it. Everywhere we turn we are constantly assaulted
with news of impending danger . . . whether it's possible
acts of terrorism, deadly diseases, kids that kill, environmental disasters, food contamination . . . and I could go
on. No wonder we have trouble embracing uncertainty
. . . there only seems to be danger ahead!

Of course, all of the above needs to be appropriately
addressed, but I suggest that the threats of our demise are
greatly exaggerated and/or erroneously reported by the
bearers of all the bad news. In my opinion, the news on
television is one of the worst offenders. There is a
desperate need for creating drama out of the drab that
hopefully will keep us watching. Reporters and their
"pseudo-experts" on the evening news go from one nightmare story to the next and we can now get twenty-four
hours a day of disaster on our twenty-four hour news
channels. We should congratulate ourselves that we still
have the courage to walk out the door!

Are you asking yourself, "Just where did all the good
news go?" Trust me, the good news is there, it's all around

us. It's just that the bad news seems to get all the attention. As we watch the negative news droning on and on and on, it's important that we keep in mind this important truth . . .

We in Western society live amazingly wonderful lives!

Really, we do! Let me just skim the surface . . .

- Most of us eat very well—too well, if our obsession with dieting is any indication!
- We live much longer than human beings have ever lived before.
- We can effectively control so many diseases with the miracles of modern and alternative medicine.
- Most of us live in a free society.
- Our world has expanded incredibly through the miracles of technology.
- More than ever before, people are traveling far and wide to explore this big, wide, beautiful world.
- Flowers bloom, mountains soar, and skies give us a changing masterpiece every day of the year.
- Throughout the world, millions and millions of people perform intensely beautiful, generous, loving and caring acts.
- And what is most encouraging . . . the world is filled with wondrous possibility and the ever-present opportunity to change what is Bad News into what is Good News.

I'm sure you could add a few of your own favorites to the list. Can you see that in so many ways . . . ALL IS WELL? In fact, in many ways, we are better off than we have ever been. Yet if we paid attention only to the bad news in the media and the bad news in our minds, we would think that we had died and gone to Hell. Who wouldn't be in a state of paralyzing fright? The fact is . . . there is so much good news around us that it would stagger the imagination, that is, IF WE PAID ATTENTION!

While it's true that we can't control the bad news fed to us by so many sources in the outside world, we can certainly control the bad news we allow into our mind. But as you may have already discovered, creating a Good News World in your mind isn't as easy as one would think it should be. Our minds seem to be addicted to bad news and you know how difficult it is to overcome addictions. Our assignment now is to become addicted to good news. Since we won't find much help in the outside world, it's up to us to help ourselves.

Embracing Uncertainty has many suggestions as to how to create the Good News Habit. Here is just one example to make you think about the wonderful possibilities:

Become an "observer" instead of becoming trapped in the drama. The concept of the observer is an important one to understand. When we become the observer, we take ourselves one step away from the drama and we watch, instead of becoming caught up in it all. Becoming the observer also allows us to let go of expectations and to create a sense of wonder instead of fear about the future. "I wonder how this will all turn out?" Like an interesting movie unfolding.

There is something else that becoming the observer allows us to do and that is to become a perpetual student—always learning and always growing. Let me show you how this works. Let's imagine that we are bombarded with news of a potential environmental crisis. Instead of becoming caught up in the drama, we can see ourselves as students studying the why's and wherefore's of the environment. We may also investigate what we can do to help, such as how we can change our lifestyle to improve the situation.

So instead of, "Help! I pray it won't affect ME!", it becomes, "Hmm. I wonder how this will all turn out and if there is anything I can do to help." The first is a closing, a tensing of the muscles as a feeling of helplessness kicks in. The second is an opening, a willingness to learn and grow . . . and a willingness to participate in the solution.

This is healthy for our own lives and for the environment as well. If we see it all as education and participation, our minds can operate in a much more constructive fashion. Education and participation . . . not fear and frustration.

So become an observer and student of the world around you. In this way life becomes exciting, challenging, and filled with meaning and purpose. This is watching the bad news in a good news frame of mind. Come to think of it, what an exhilarating way to go through life!

This is just one way to watch the news without getting upset. Just remember . . . we can't control what's out there . . . but, in all aspects of life, we can definitely learn to control what's inside our heads. And that's really the only control we need.

© 2002 Susan Jeffers, Ph.D.

(For much more go to *Embracing Uncertainty*)

41.

But You Promised!

IT WAS VERY EARLY IN OUR RELATIONSHIP. And when the most wonderful man I had ever known lied to me about something in his past, I was devastated. The incident in his past didn't both me at all . . . his lying about it did. His cries of "I was afraid you'd really be upset if you found out" only seemed to make my disdain grow. I self-righteously accused him of being a pathetic coward. My hurt and disappointment were so intense that I almost ended the relationship on the spot. Thankfully, experience had taught me not to make such a rash decision in such an agitated state.

Over the next few days, I despaired with the realization that I could no longer trust him completely. My rage was uncontrollable at times. And so was my sadness. After all, if he deceived me once, he could do it again. And how could I love someone I couldn't trust? Haven't we been taught that trust is one of the most important ingredients of a relationship?

Another disturbing question lurked in the depths of my despair. He really was an incredibly wonderful person. I knew he cared deeply. I knew our relationship was important to him. I knew that in the depths of his being, he really wanted what was best for me. I asked myself, given all this, IF I COULDN'T TRUST HIM . . . WHO COULD I TRUST? My moment of enlightenment came when a voice from within answered . . . PROBABLY NO ONE!

I really didn't want to hear that. The implications were too upsetting: If total trust was one of my conditions for a relationship, I would probably be alone for the rest of my life. How depressing!

After drowning in my upset for a while, I decided that a convent was definitely not my style and I had better rethink the situation. After all, there are definite advantages to being in a relationship, especially with him. Maybe our emphasis on trust tends to be a bit overdone . . . especially when it comes to our mates. From them we expect it 100%. Maybe expecting 100% of anything from another human being is asking for trouble. I relaxed a bit. A glimmer of light was emerging from the darkness. Maybe if I could change my thinking, I wouldn't have to change my man!

I began by asking myself who else do I know who has been guilty of telling a lie or two. My mind immediately went back to the time my children were very young. They lied all the time . . . blatantly. Nothing subtle about them. "We did NOT break the ashtray . . . the turtle did!" I even considered recording their lies for posterity . . . they were so clever. I reminded myself that I never stopped loving them when they lied. Trying to be the model of a perfect mother, I pointed out the evil of their ways. Underneath, however, I chuckled to myself with the understanding that kids will be kids. It just never occurred to me that ADULTS WILL BE KIDS AS WELL when they are frightened of losing something they value and, at such times, may tell a lie or two to protect themselves.

I then looked into my mirror and asked, "Mirror, mirror on the wall, who is the most honest of us all?" The mirror responded that it was probably some little old man in the heart of Kansas, but IT CERTAINLY WAS NOT ME! The mirror found me out. Yes, I had told a few lies in my time to save my hide. And had I told Mark EVERY-THING about my past? Indeed I did . . . well, except for those things I didn't want him to know. And although I tried valiantly, I could not come up with any great "spiri-tual" explanation for my lying. I finally had to admit that I was simply playing the same game as he had played—self-preservation.

The mirror revealed something else. If the truth be known, I was feeling a definite sense of relief underneath all my self-righteous rage. I think it had something to do with freedom. I had been working very hard to approach this relationship with an unnatural degree of perfection. It was beginning to feel oppressive—like a life sentence. It's very limiting when you try to be perfect. My discovery of his lie let me out of my self-imposed jail—allowed me to be human as well. I don't mean this in a vindictive sense, but purely in the sense of, "Hey, we all make mistakes." Trying to maintain impossible standards for ourselves creates an intense feeling of being trapped!

I was beginning to make progress. Maybe total trust . . . or total anything . . . is not within the bounds of reason. Forgiveness was right around the bend as I began to see that I might have been asking the impossible. But it did make me ponder why trust is given so much weight in a relationship. One could blame it on a number of factors, such as a need to possess, a need to control, fear of being conned, low self-esteem, and so on. . . . all of which boils down to a basic insecurity that seems to be universal in the human species. One characteristic of insecurity is that it often demands a guarantee . . . often in situations where a guarantee is impossible.

The wedding ceremony offers a perfect example. There are people marrying for the second or third or more times still uttering the words "until death do us part". Are they serious? Haven't they learned by their own experience that life doesn't work that way. Wouldn't it be more honest for them to say that they will love, honor and . . . whatever . . . until it doesn't work for them anymore . . . however long that may be? But who wants to ruin their marriage ceremony with truth? We all want the guarantee.

Even with my awareness of all this, my own need for security still prompts me, every now and then, to ask Mark stupid questions such as "Will you love me forever?" Being sensitive to my needs, he obliges with a tender, "Of course I will". Music to my ears, even though I'm subliminally aware that it would be more honest for him to tell me, "At this moment I feel I will love you forever." He needn't even add the logical sentence that would follow. "Who can predict what the future holds?" This is honest. That I can trust . . . but do I really want to hear that? Absolutely not! I want the guarantee . . . even if it is a "lie".

If insecurity is at the root of our unrealistic expectations, and I believe it is, the answer to the problems relating to trust is self-evident. It lies in getting to the place deep within us all that understands that there really is no one we totally can trust . . . except ourselves. I don't mean trusting ourselves to never tell a lie, I mean trusting our ability to handle whatever anyone says or does to us.

Let me repeat this important reality:

THE ONLY THING WE CAN SAFELY TRUST IS OUR ABILITY TO HANDLE WHATEVER ANYONE SAYS OR DOES TO US!

Really emblazon this thought in your mind. For in this kind of thinking lies our sense of inner peace. No longer do we have to control the actions or thoughts of the men or women in our lives. No longer do we have to feel outraged or betrayed when they change their minds. Whatever happens relative to the people in our lives, we will be able to handle it.

Aside from our peace of mind, there are definite advantages to this kind of thinking. In the first place, we can breathe a sign of relief knowing we won't have to retreat to a convent for the rest of our lives. And while this new attitude may take a little romance out of our lives, we shouldn't feel disillusioned. On the contrary, we can feel wiser and in much better control of our lives and our relationship. The mere debunking of the fairy tale expectation of perfect trust creates a healthier and more compassionate way of relating. When we really trust ourselves, the fear goes away . . . and what's left is the love.

As for me, I guess I'll always want him to tell me he'll love me forever. It does sound divine. But my heart will rest a little easier knowing I DON'T HAVE TO HOLD HIM TO IT. We are a race of imperfect individuals and while he is a beautiful person, he is, after all, human. If we want to keep it in the realm of the fairy tale . . . my prince has gained back a few characteristics of the frog, but frogs are really loveable once you get to know them. And now that my mirror has revealed my own frog-like tendencies,

I realize that I would not really be compatible with a fairy-tale prince anyway. So you see, everything works out just as it's supposed to . . . not necessarily how we imagined it . . . but exactly as it's supposed to.

© 1983, 1989 Susan Jeffers, Ph.D.

(To learn much more about trust in a relationship, read *Opening Our Hearts to Men* and *The Feel the Fear Guide to Lasting Love*.)

42.

I Wish . . .

ON A VISIT TO NEW YORK a few years ago, I was fortunate enough to see an enchanting Broadway musical entitled *Into the Woods.*[1] Ironically, I never would have chosen to see this particular play as it was all about fairy tales . . . a subject matter that normally wouldn't be of interest to me. But on our arrival in New York, my wonderful sister and brother-in-law surprised us with the tickets. And I'm so happy they did as there are few Broadway shows that I have enjoyed as much I enjoyed this one.

Into the Woods was so entertaining and deep . . . deep . . . deep as it cleverly depicted so much of what we all experience in our Journey through life. This includes the good, the bad, the beautiful, the ugly, the sad, the happy . . . and more. I loved the clever interaction of our popular fairy-tale characters as they adventured in and out of the woods. These fairy-tale characters included Cinderella, her Prince, her wicked stepmother and stepsisters, Jack and his famous bean stalk, Rapunzel and her long hair, the witch, the baker and his wife, Little Red Riding Hood and the wolf, and a few other characters effectively thrown into the mix.

And what exactly are "the woods?" The woods are portrayed as not only a rich forest, but more significantly, a deep, dark and sometimes dangerous place where we find life, death, adventure, surprise, answers, confusion, clarity, sadness, exploration . . . all those things that make life rich and difficult at the same time. Throughout our lives, we often find it necessary to go into the woods to find the answers to questions that burn in our hearts. And we leave the woods when clarity is reached . . . only to return when we find ourselves confused once again. And that certainly does seem to be the pattern of life after all—confusion to clarity, confusion to clarity, confusion to clarity . . . and so it goes.

What often sends many of us into the woods is our dissatisfaction with the way things are. So too, each of the homes of the characters in the play was filled with "wishes" . . . as are our own homes. I wish . . . for a child. I wish . . . for a relationship. I wish . . . for money. I wish . . . for excitement. In the grand scheme of things, "wishes" often lead to disappointment. But if we can let go of our need for things to turn out a certain way, our wishes can send us into the woods to discover many things about ourselves and about the world that we can discover in no other way.

One important lesson we learn is that even when wishes are fulfilled, there is always more to wish for. And sometimes, even if our wishes are fulfilled, we are not necessarily happy. But with one eye on the learning, we can always be enriched. As an example, in the play Cinderella dreamt of marrying the Prince. Ultimately she won the Prince's heart, married him, and realized that because of his roving eye, he was not the man for her. She would have to look elsewhere for love. She went from rags to riches, but realized that true happiness in life, may come from "somewhere in between." She decided . . .

> Going for "nothing" doesn't work. Going for "everything" doesn't work. "Somewhere in between" can be a great place to live our lives . . . in fact, it could be Heaven.

What a great lesson!

The play beautifully portrays how nothing ever stays the same. We might think we have life exactly the way we want to have it. And, BAM, something changes. We can't hold on. On the other hand, things could be horrible. We may think there is no hope. And, BAM, something changes. And all is well. We can't hold onto the good . . . or the bad. It's just all part of the journey.

And, if we are wise, it is in the woods that we can learn, we can grow and we can shine. We are encouraged, discouraged, saddened, emboldened and wiser for it all. But the trick is to go "into the woods" without regret as to what we find . . . or don't find. That we made the effort is enough . . . providing that, along the way, we expand the essence of who we are. Of course, some of us do; some of us don't. We must always remember that it's all a choice.

The play ends with a very beautiful song telling us "No one is alone." And it is true. We all have our own wishes, which take us in and out of the woods time and time again as we explore the many aspects of this HUGE life that we are living. We are all trying to find meaning in it all, trying to reach the best of who we are, trying to fill ourselves up with a deep sense of power and love, trying to love and be loved . . . each in our own way. Understanding this, we know that when we look into the eyes of everyone around us, we truly are not alone.

As I said earlier, *Into the Woods* was not a play that I would have chosen . . . but I'm so happy that fate (and my sister and brother-in-law!) chose it for me. A lot of the great things in life happen that way. Have you noticed?

© 2003 Susan Jeffers, Ph.D.

43.

A Party Idea That Can Change Your Life

THE BEST PARTY I EVER ATTENDED was in the year 1986 . . . and it was called the "1991 Party." Let me explain.

This wonderful evening was created by members of a very forward-looking and loving group that Mark and I belonged to in Los Angeles called The Inside Edge.[1] The premise of the party was as follows:

- We all had to envision what we would like to have happen in our lives five years into the future—which in our case was 1991.
- After we created our vision, we were then to "stretch," that is, to make our vision much more than we actually thought we could accomplish.
- When we came to the party, we were all to act-as-if it really was 1991 and our vision had come true. That means we were to dress the part, talk the part and come with "props" demonstrating our amazing journey to the achievement of our vision between the years 1986 and 1991.

- In addition to talking about our own success, we were to applaud the success of everyone else as well.

As you can imagine this was a perfect scenario for an evening of congratulations, excitement, laughter, fun . . . and creativity!

I remember that one man's vision was to be a multi-millionaire giving away money to others by the year 1991. He came to the party dressed as a "beach bum" (his dream of retirement) and he was handing out money (in the form of lottery tickets) to everyone at the party. One woman brought a mock TIME magazine with her face emblazoned on the cover. Her vision was winning an international award for being responsible for many advances in the peace movement. One woman came with a large sandwich board on which were painted the images of her new husband and two children, all of which she envisioned creating by the year 1991. My husband, who produced *I Claudius* and other memorable series for television, came in evening clothes having envisioned it was the premiere of the first co-production with the Russians. The range of creativity was amazing.

What did I envision? In 1986, I was embarking on a career as a writer. As yet, I had not succeeded in getting my first book accepted by a publisher. My stretch for the party was that three book contracts would be signed by the year 1991. (Mind you, I would have been happy if one book contract had been signed!) In the spirit of the party, I showed up with three mock books. Throughout the evening, I "fabricated" a story about the incredible success of my books. I even told my remarkable story of success to a video camera that recorded it for all posterity . . . as did everyone else.

It was an evening of people supporting each other in their dreams. As Mark and I went around the room congratulating everyone on their successes, we, too, were bombarded with congratulations. As part of this scenario, I remember someone came up to me congratulating me on my bestseller, telling me that she saw me on four television shows. Another congratulated me for winning the Pulitzer Prize. There was a lot of laughter and hugs. What was most significant to me was that by the end of the evening, I actually believed that creating three books by the year 1991 was a definite possibility!!! Why not? It was no longer a stretch. And what did happen by the year 1991? You guessed it. I actually did create three successful books—with a fourth one on the way! It's amazing what that this one party did for me!

Of course, not everyone's vision was realized in the same way that mine was. They were obviously meant to travel a different path than they envisioned. But for me, that special evening gave me the strength and confidence to strongly commit to a successful career in writing. And I do believe it was this strong commitment that made my vision of the future actually happen. Commitment is a powerful force, indeed!

© 1995 Susan Jeffers, Ph.D.

44.

Escalating Violence: What Do We Tell the Children?

WE LIVE IN A TIME of escalating uncertainty. No doubt about it. And in my travels, I am frequently asked, "What do I tell my children when they express concerns about all the violence in the world?"

Certainly, in our role as parents, teachers, or caregivers, we watch as our children are shaken up by the inescapable barrage of scary news involving death, bombs, fighting, enemies and the like. They are frightened and confused as they ask questions such as: "Am I safe?" "Will the bombs ever come here?" "Why do people kill each other?" Even if we choose to keep our television sets turned off, a sense of fear and unrest seems to be hovering in the air.

So what do you tell the children to comfort them as they ask many of the same questions that you, at times, have asked yourself? Here are a few suggestions . . .

You can tell them:

"It's okay to be afraid. Everyone has times when they are afraid, even me. But our fears need not stop us from acting in ways that are powerful and loving. Our fears need not stop us from becoming the best we can be. Our fears need not stop us from reaching out and helping others. And as we act in ways that are powerful and loving, and as we try to become the best we can be, and as we reach out and help others, guess what happens . . . our fears get smaller and smaller and smaller. Let's work on this together."

All that is happening in the world offers you and your children a great opportunity to talk, learn, share, imagine, plan, and open up to each other. Use it all . . . the good and the bad . . . to make the connection between you grow in a healthy and enduring way.

You can tell them . . .

"None of us knows what the future holds, but I do know that whatever happens, you will handle it. You may not know it yet, but you have a HUGE amount of strength within you that will allow you to handle anything that happens. So whenever your head is filled with bad thoughts about the future, just keep repeating over and over again . . .

No matter what happens, I can handle it!
No matter what happens, I can handle it!
No matter what happens, I can handle it!

Let's practice this together."

It is clear to me that the frequent repetition of this wonderful affirmation can eventually quiet the "what if's" in your children's minds that make them feel insecure, frightened and weak. Because I believe that this is such a valuable affirmation for children to learn, I created, with my friend Donna Gradstein, a book for young children entitled *I Can Handle It*.[1] It contains many stories of children handling all sorts of things, each in their own way . . . and gaining a greater sense of confidence in the process. So when your children express any fears about the future, just remind them to say over and over again, "Whatever happens, I'll handle it!" I suggest you say it right along with them. Young or old, knowing we can handle all that happens in our lives gives us a wonderful sense of comfort.

You can tell them . . .

"I know you are confused by people angrily arguing with each other about many things in this world. You are wondering who is right? And who is wrong? In this very complicated world, I don't believe anybody can know for sure. I believe that most people truly want the very same things . . . peace and love in this world. They just see different ways of finding peace and love. What we need to do is to stop arguing and start listening carefully to each other. Maybe we won't change our minds about what we believe, but with open ears and an open heart, we truly can learn a lot."

I see this as a wonderful opportunity to teach your children that we all need to open our hearts and minds to those who believe differently than we do. You need to explain that if we walked in someone else's shoes, perhaps we would see many things their way instead of our way. In truth, we live in a "maybe" world. Maybe we're right; maybe we're wrong. Nobody knows the "Grand Design," the bigger picture that none of us can see. Given that, as we unblock our ears, we might learn a lot and develop a warmer feeling towards those who have a reason to think differently than we do. That's a very good reason for unblocking our ears!

You can tell them:

"I know the news is very scary. But there are also good things happening all around us. Let's create a list of all the good things that are happening and, every day, add to the list. I think that our list will get very, very, very long! In fact, let's see how long a list of good things we can make."

We live in a "bad news world", no doubt about it. We see and hear bad news everywhere we turn. But you can work with your children to create a "good news world". Certainly the above challenge of seeing how long a list of good things they can make is a great way to begin.

On this list could be all the good things they see people doing for others. Also on the list could be all the good things they experience in their lives . . . food on the table, a soothing, hot bath, people who care about them, toys, friends, teachers, and on and on and on. As you can see, this is a wonderful opportunity to create a joyful inner life of abundance for your children. It stands to reason that as children focus on the good, by definition, they will have much less time to focus on the bad, thereby seeing the world in a less frightening way.

You can tell them . . .

"We can all do our part in making this a more loving world. Why don't we each think of ten things we can do to spread our love around . . . and then, let's do them . . . one at a time. I bet when we finish, we will want to think of ten more things we can do. It feels so good when we do our part in making this a more loving world."

Positive action is a great confidence builder and there are many ways that children can get involved in making this a more loving world. After the attack on the World Trade Center, I remember seeing children raising money for the needy with their lemonade stands, writing letters to children who had lost someone they loved, and so on.

There are also ways that children can be more loving in terms of their own behavior . . . thereby bringing more love into the family, their school, their community, and into the world. You can tell them what Stewart, one of the *I Can Handle It* kids that Donna and I created, has to say about it:

"I don't understand why wars happen. I just don't understand it at all. But, I can handle it.

Maybe there isn't enough love in the world and that's why people fight with each other. Maybe I don't act loving some of the time. In fact, a lot of the time! When I am being mean to my sister, I am not being loving. When I am fighting with my brother, I am not being loving. When I want more Christmas presents than everyone else, I am not being loving. When I say, "I hate you" to someone, I am not being loving.

Maybe I have to start being more loving. If everyone acted more loving, maybe there wouldn't be any more wars. You know what? I think everyone's love counts. Even mine . . . and yours! See . . . *we can handle it!*

No matter what happens, we can handle it![2]

Oh, if all our children learned the lesson that Stewart learned, we would have a lot more happy children . . . and parents!

All of the above are just suggestions as to what you can begin to tell your children. Of course, you will want to adapt these ideas to your own situation, your own beliefs and your own children.

None of us wants a world filled with conflict. But that is what the world is handing us right now. And we would be wise to find ways of creating something positive and enriching out of it all. Certainly one way of doing this is to show your children how they can lessen their fears . . . how they can be more loving . . . and how they can truly make a difference in this world. The good news is that as we teach our children these valuable lessons, we teach ourselves as well.

© 2003 Susan Jeffers, Ph.D.

45.

Give Me a Higher Love!

SO MANY PEOPLE IN TODAY'S WORLD are troubled by the unsuccessful relationships they have with the partners in their lives. Yet, I believe that within each and every one of us lies the ability to create what I call a Higher Love . . . a love that transcends the pettiness of every day life and lifts us into a state of joy and abundance. When we radiate the essence of this Higher Love into our relationships, they are magically transformed.

Let me give just a few of the guidelines I have discovered for creating such a Higher Love, understanding that it may take a while to get into the groove . . . but with each step of the way, our ability to love and be loved gets better and better and better . . .

1) A Higher Love begins with a love of humanity. The more we succeed as a "lover" in the world outside our relationship, the more we will succeed as a lover inside our relationship. Our life has to be about creating a context for love, which touches everything and everyone around us.

2) A Higher Love focuses on essence rather than form. We notice the blessings our mate brings into our lives . . . not on the fact that he or she leaves the bathroom in a mess.

3) A Higher Love is about learning. It includes most of the same emotions as a "lower" love . . . anger, judgment, self-righteousness and so on. The difference is that in a Higher Love, we pick up the mirror (Why am I reacting this way and what can I do about it?) instead of the magnifying glass (Why is he (or she) doing this?), using these emotions as keys to self-discovery, not as tools to bash our mate.

4) A Higher Love is intentional. Knowing that the natural state for something left unattended is deterioration, we ask ourselves daily . . . "What can I do to nourish this love today?" And then we proceed to do it!

5) A Higher Love invites touching, but not attachment. We become our own person. When we cling to another, we become their person . . . and soon we begin to hate.

6) A Higher Love is committed. The essence of this commitment is that we honor our agreements in whatever form they take and that we love, respect, care for, and support the growth of the beautiful person over which we have been given emotional guardianship.

7) A Higher Love is filled with appreciation. We are generous with our thanks. "Thank you" is a good first

step toward creating a transcendent relationship. "Thank you for contributing so much to my life." "Thank you for supporting who I am." "Thank you for sharing my life." "Thank you." "Thank you." "Thank you."

8) A Higher Love is uplifting. As guardian over our loved-one's feelings, we lift him (or her) up when his belief in himself falters. In so doing we lift ourselves up as well.

While the above is an ideal which may seem to lie beyond our present reach, the mere focusing on the principles of a Higher Love will slowly help us to understand what real love looks like. And as we act on this understanding, we will create the beautiful kind of love we are all seeking. Trust me on this one.

(Whether you are a man or woman, you can learn much more about creating a Higher Love in *Opening Our Hearts to Men* and *The Feel the Fear Guide to Lasting Love*.)

46.

For a Brief Moment in Time

I WAS SITTING ON THE PROMENADE on a beautiful sunny day drinking a cappuccino and eating a chocolate almond bar looking up at the blue, blue sky. *For a brief moment in time, I thought I had died and gone to heaven.*

I was at dinner with my husband, Mark, and a few wonderful friends. There was love, good food and drink, lively conversation and much laughter. *For a brief moment in time, I thought I had died and gone to heaven.*

I went for a walk and noticed a bed of the most exquisite fuchsia flowers I had ever seen. They took my breath away. *For a brief moment in time, I thought I had died and gone to heaven.*

My son cooked a Mother's Day meal with the help of my daughter and son-in-law. As we sat around the dinner table, I felt a deep sense of happiness as I looked at my beautiful children all grown up. They raised their glasses and thanked me for being such a great mother. *For a brief moment in time, I thought I had died and gone to heaven.*

My day's work was done. I joined Mark on the deck to watch the sunset. It was beautiful beyond belief. All I could utter was, "Wow! Thank you, God!" *For a brief moment in time, I thought I had died and gone to heaven.*

I watched an amazing film. It captured my imagination and changed my life in an exquisite way. I was moved to tears. *For a brief moment in time, I thought I had died and gone to heaven.*

I was driving up Pacific Coast Highway with my windows wide open and my music playing loudly . . . Bon Jovi and his elevating song, "It's My Life." I felt so alive and free. *For a brief moment in time, I thought I had died and gone to heaven.*

It was raining outside with the raindrops softly hitting the deck. I was lying in bed, warm and content, reading a good book . . . one of my favorite light-hearted mysteries. How cozy it was. *For a brief moment in time, I thought I had died and gone to heaven.*

I was sitting at my desk writing a chapter for my newest book. At one point in time, I felt myself sailing on a wave of creativity . . . totally absorbed in the process of bringing words to life. Awesome. *For a brief moment in time, I thought I had died and gone to heaven.*

I was on the telephone with my sister. We laughed and pondered and planned and shared our hearts with each other as we always do . . . and then we laughed some more. A much loved voice on the other end of the phone. *For a brief moment in time, I thought I had died and gone to heaven.*

I was speaking to a large group of people in London. There was a moment when we connected magically. They touched me and I touched them. It felt as though the world stood still. *For a brief moment in time, I thought I had died and gone to heaven.*

It was a plane ride from Texas to Los Angeles. We took off in a maze of clouds. We climbed and climbed. At one point the sky lightened as we broke through the clouds into the bright sunlight. Magnificent! *For a brief moment in time, I thought I had died and gone to heaven.*

It was my birthday and friends and family gathered together at an amazing party Mark arranged in my honor. I felt blessed to have so many people from the many areas of my life gathered together to celebrate this special occasion with me. The love in the room was tangible and I felt it deeply. *For a brief moment in time, I thought I had died and gone to heaven.*

I was walking in the park. A homeless old man approached me and I gave him some money. He asked if he could give me a hug. I said, of course. It felt so good. We both cried with the greatness of human connection. *For a brief moment in time, I thought I had died and gone to heaven.*

It was late. I was tired. It felt so good to climb into bed with my wonderful Mark. We cuddled. We said, "I love you" to each other. I began to fall asleep with a deep sense of peace and happiness. *For a brief moment in time, I thought I had died and gone to heaven.*

So many of us wonder if we will go to Heaven when we die. It occurs to me that in so many ways we have already arrived. We just need to notice.

© 2002 Susan Jeffers, Ph.D.

A Holiday Trilogy

Family get-togethers during the holiday season can be a very difficult time for many of us. Whatever holiday your family celebrates, the following three articles were written to help you make the catch-phrase "Happy Holidays" a reality.

Happy Holidays!

47.

Creating Holiday Blessings

FOR MANY OF US, the family getting together for the holidays is a joy; for many others, it is a time of intense upset. Whichever is true for you, now is the time to CHOOSE to create a very valuable and loving holiday experience for all concerned. And trust me when I tell you that it is your choice. Here are a few valuable bits of information about holiday blessings:

1) *Let go of your pictures of what the holidays are supposed to look like.* We all want the holidays to look a certain way . . . loving, close, warm, festive and joyful. And when this idyllic picture eludes us, we are very disappointed. The reality is some families flow together; others fight together. If your family tends to belong in the latter category, then don't expect them to be any different this year. "Well, Susan, if my family continues to "fight together" this year, then how can is it possible to create a valuable and loving holiday experience?" Keep reading.

2) *Stop trying to change other people.* You may want everyone in your life to follow *your* perfect "script", not theirs. One of my favorite quotes is "Never try to teach a pig to sing. It wastes your time and it annoys the pig." Now, this doesn't mean people in your life are pigs; it means stop trying to change the nature of other people. Work only on yourself. .

Instead of trying to change someone, despite how he or she is behaving, just send loving light to that person. You can't imagine the profound effect it has on others when you project your love onto them. As you continue to project your love onto others, you will ultimately melt into the realization that we are all human beings doing the best we can. And from this place, compassion for others . . . and for ourselves . . . is born.

3) *Pick up the mirror instead of the magnifying glass.* Perhaps the behavior of certain family members is inappropriate. But what about your reactions? Are they appropriate? It is very important to remember for the holidays (and forever!) that the only thing we can effectively control is our REACTION to what happens around us. Sending love to others is a wonderful "reaction" to others . . . despite what they are doing.

When you pick up the mirror, you get answers to such important questions as: "Why does it always upset me when my mother nags me about giving her a grandchild?" (A much better question than "Why does my mother always ask me that stupid question?") Or "Why does my brother drive me crazy when he just sits there and lets my mother and me do everything?" (Again, a much better question than "How can my brother be so rude and insensitive?") When we focus on our reactions to others, self-knowledge is born and we are able to make healing changes in our lives. This is taking control of our lives instead of living as weak and helpless victims.

It's not that the behavior of others is always right; it's that we hurt only ourselves by letting their behavior take away our peace of mind. Also, we lose our ability to reach out in love when we are constantly in judgment of others. To let others be who they are and reach out to them anyway is the height of loving others.

4) *Focus on the Abundance Instead of the Lack.* Yes, there are many things we may want to change about our relatives and friends. But, it is important to take our eyes off of the negative and focus on the positive.

What are some positive things to appreciate? That we HAVE a family to get annoyed at (some people aren't that lucky). That we have food on the table. That we have an opportunity to learn more about becoming a loving person. And on and on and on.

I know it is very hard to focus on the positive at times, especially when we are being criticized or annoyed by those we love. So start practicing the art of appreciation RIGHT NOW! Notice everything wonderful in your life, big or small, and write all this "wonderfulness" down in a Journal. Some of you will recognize it as "The Book of Abundance" I talk about in *Feel the Fear and Do It Anyway.* If you start now, you may have broken the destructive habit of focusing only on the bad by the time the holidays come around. Focusing on abundance is a habit *well worth acquiring*.

5) *Focus on the Giving*. You will be a far happier person if your question for the holidays is "What am I going to give?" instead of "What am I going to get?"

What do you have to give? Certainly your love. You can radiate love to everyone around you. Even when someone is upsetting you greatly, you project the thought "I love you. I love you. I love you." That is a wonderful gift.

What else can you give? Goodies you selected with care and sensitivity. Give gifts you can afford and the key is to expect nothing in return. If you get something in return, especially something you love, that's wonderful. If you don't, that's wonderful, too. Remember, your purpose is to "give it away", not exchange.

What else can you give? You can give your commitment to be there 100% helping and participating in anyway you can. We do this not only for others, but for ourselves as well. Too many of us spend time with our family and friends wishing we were somewhere else, thereby missing an important opportunity to understand how important we truly are to those around us. Without this understanding, our self-esteem suffers enormously.

We must constantly ask ourselves the critical question, "If I were really important here, what would I be doing?" and then "Do it!" As you conduct your life this way, you eventually live into the understanding of how really important you are, not only to family and friends, but to the entire world around you.

I promise you that if you are truly giving it away, expecting nothing in return, you will feel wonderful! Remember that the enjoyment of the holidays begins and ends with caring, sharing, having compassion for others, and radiating love.

6) *Lighten Up.* As I talk about in *End the Struggle and Dance With Life*, learn how to "wear the world like a loose garment." Wiggle around and feel free to enjoy it all . . . just as it is. That *is* the height of freedom and happiness.

The above will take you a long way toward creating a magical holiday. (You may have already realized that these holiday tips are the ingredients of, not just a beautiful holiday, but of a beautiful life.) Of course, some practice may be needed as you possibly have to break a lot of "unhappy holiday habits" before you can take in the beauty all around you. Here is where your mirror comes in handy.

When you pick up the mirror instead of the magnifying glass, you learn where you are still stuck in terms of your neediness for things to be a certain way. And little by little, you learn how to let go. When you pick up the mirror, you learn where you have a hard time giving . . . and little by little, giving becomes easier and easier. When you pick up the mirror, you learn how hard it is to focus on the good instead of the bad. And little by little, you learn how to take in all the beauty around you.

Remember to have PATIENCE. Don't beat yourself up if your loving nature disappears at times. Just keep patting yourself on the back with every forward step you take.

By the way, even if you don't have a family to spend the holidays with, not to worry! The above tips will stand you in good stead. (You might think about volunteering to help the needy . . . there are so many people in the world who need your love!) Just keep spreading your love around . . . and love will find you in the most unexpected ways.

Here's a summary: Whatever your situation, it is important to learn how to . . .

- Let go of the expectations and make something wonderful from what is.
- Stop trying to change other people.
- Pick up the mirror and learn how to control your reactions to all things in your life.
- Focus on the abundance instead of the lack.
- Focus on the giving instead of the getting.
- Lighten up.
- Be patient with yourself . . . and others.

A tried-and-true formula for a wonderful holiday . . . and a wonderful life!

© 2000 Susan Jeffers, Ph.D.

48.

Instant Angels

MANY YEARS AGO, I decided to travel from New York City, which was my home at the time, to attend a week-long workshop at Esalen Institute, a Spiritual center located a few hours drive from San Francisco in Big Sur, California. With great excitement about the upcoming week, I flew into San Francisco, rented a car, and began my drive south to the magnificent Highway 1 which runs along the California coast.

I wasn't in the car any longer than ten minutes when the skies darkened and the rains came down fast and furious. It was a difficult drive, to say the least, but my mind kept focusing on the wonderful workshop I would soon be attending.

When I finally arrived in an area that I knew was just about eleven miles north of Esalen, I thought to myself, "It won't be too long now." So you can imagine my disappointment to see a barrier in the road as I drove a little further that said "ROAD CLOSED . . . FLOODING AHEAD". What a blow! Since it was the only road that leads to Eslalen, I knew I wasn't going to get to the beginning of my workshop in time.

It's then that I made a downright stupid decision. I said to myself, "The road's probably not too bad. They're just being overly cautious." I then proceeded to go around the warning signs and continued on my way. Stupid, indeed! As I drove, I noticed I was the only car on the road—for an obvious reason: All the other drivers were wise enough to obey the "ROAD CLOSED" sign!

For those of you who've never driven the splendid Highway 1, let me explain that, in the area of Big Sur, it is a twisting road with many turns that, at the time, had no guard rails to stop one from accidentally hurtling down to the cliffs and the ocean below. So you can understand why I began to feel a bit uneasy as I surveyed what I had gotten myself into. But I just kept driving.

Suddenly I was aware of a strange sensation. Instead of moving forward, I could feel the car being lifted as it slowly began "floating" toward the edge of the cliff. What had looked just like the road ahead was actually a big crevice in the road filled with water! In a strangely calm state of mind, I thought to myself, "This is the end! I'm going over the cliff!" I tried opening the door but with no luck; the water was so high that it was blocking the door. I was trapped.

And then it happened. At that very critical moment in time, a highway patrol tow truck rounded the corner. The driver immediately saw what was happening, quickly ran out of the truck, attached a rope to my car, and pulled me and the car to safety . . . thereby saving my life. What makes this all the more remarkable is the fact that Highway 1 stretches for miles and miles and the likelihood of that tow truck coming around the corner just as I needed it was remote, to put it mildly. In fact, I put it in the category of "Miracle" . . . and I put the tow truck driver in the category of "Instant Angel".

I might add that he was an Instant Angel who couldn't stop cursing at me, calling me an idiot for disregarding the sign, and telling me if I didn't go back to the area behind the warning signs and stay there until it was safe to proceed, he would have me arrested and thrown in jail! (Instant Angels come in all forms.) I meekly apologized, sheepishly thanked him, and headed back wondering how I could have been so reckless. An important lesson learned: When it comes to personal safety, there are times to "Feel the Fear . . . and DON'T Do It Anyway!"

It was a few days before the rains stopped and the road was once again passable. But, as fate would have it, it was a life-changing few days. At first I was understandably disappointed. So near and yet so far! Reluctantly, I checked myself into a cozy little inn. When hunger pains made themselves felt, I made my way to Nepenthe, an enchanting local restaurant and bar located on the cliffs overlooking the ocean. After spending a few hours there, I decided it was a wonderful place to just hang out and enjoy the crackling fireplace and the sensational view . . . which I did for the few days before the road was free and clear and ready for travelers.

Unexpectedly it was a workshop of a different kind and certainly one that I needed. (Workshops come in all forms.) I learned the pleasure of having nothing to do and nowhere to go. I spent hours just looking at the view and happily passing time with interesting people. I laughed a lot. I appreciated a lot. I ate a lot! In fact, I am convinced that I learned more about what I needed to learn there than I could have learned at the workshop I was supposed to be attending. (It's all happening perfectly!) I then realized that the flooded road was a blessing in disguise.

Much time has passed and I have never stopped thinking about my tow-truck Angel who kept me from going over the cliff so many years ago. I asked myself, "Was my rescuer really an "Instant Angel"? Or was the fact that he rounded the bend just in time to save my life merely a coincidence?" While I can't offer any proof, I chose to believe that it was something more than a coincidence . . . that it had something to do with the Grand Design—the Grand Plan for our lives that our mortal minds cannot see. And, while I never learned his name, I often send my Instant Angel thanks in the form of light and love for being there when I needed him.

I also have chosen to believe that we can all be "used" by that same Universal Energy to serve as Instant Angels for others. For example, I certainly was an Instant Angel to someone recently. I was standing in a pharmacy I hardly ever frequent when I overheard an elderly women telling the pharmacist that she needed her prescription filled but didn't have her wallet with her. She explained that she needed the medicine very badly to quell her pain, but the pharmacist wouldn't fill her prescription without payment. Business is business . . . unfortunately.

Without hesitation, I said, "I'll pay for your prescription." And I pulled my credit card out of my handbag and handed it to the pharmacist. The elderly woman turned around and looked at me in amazement and exclaimed, "Are you an Angel? I just know that God sent you to me." I answered, "I never thought of myself as an Angel, but maybe God did send me to you. After all, how come I showed up here just when you needed me?" And I thought to myself, "Why did I show up at just the right time . . .

and in a place I seldom come?" Coincidence? Maybe. Maybe not. Who knows?

Yes, all of us can become Instant Angels as we step in to "rescue" others who need our help. When we do, it's as though the Light of a Higher Power comes shining right through us. And as many of you may have already discovered, the feeling is Divine.

Recently, my friend, Donna, was an Instant Angel to me. I was in bed with a virus when she called. She said that what I really needed was some home-made chicken soup . . . often jokingly referred to as Jewish penicillin. We laughed and I said that Mark and I are hopeless in the kitchen . . . no chance of home-made chicken soup here.

Three hours later, the doorbell rang and there was Donna with a pot of chicken soup hot off the stove. You can't tell me she wasn't an Instant Angel! I was so touched. In fact, I remember saying, "Donna, thank you. You're such an Angel."

As the holiday season approaches, I propose that instead of us focusing on the decorative Angels that appear on our Christmas trees and storefront windows, we put our attention on the real life Angels, seen or unseen, who make (or who have made) our lives a little easier, who protect us from harm, who are the embodiment of Love. I then propose that we thank them in any way that we can . . . a phone call, a letter, a gift, or just sending them thoughts of light and love . . . even if they are no longer with us in bodily form.

I further propose that from this moment on we embrace the role of Instant Angels and, on impulse—or with great forethought—we step in to do things for others who need our help. I can promise you a heavenly result, a feeling of joy like none else. And when someone says to you, "Thank you so much. You're such an Angel", you can bask in the glory that you truly are.

49.

Holiday Gifts of Power, Peace and Love

IN A RECENT INTERVIEW, I was asked to come up with three great gift ideas for the holiday season. That was easy for me. I love giving gifts that have to do with . . .

POWER, PEACE and LOVE

. . . all of which are necessary for a rich and beautiful life. There are so many gifts that would fall into each of these categories. Just use your wonderful imagination. As to what I would consider great gift ideas, here are a few of my favorites . . .

FOR A SENSE OF POWER . . . I love giving martial arts type of exercise tapes. I personally enjoy the Tae Bo Videotapes created by Billy Blanks. Whenever I follow along with Billy in his martial arts/boxing type exercises, I feel uplifted and certainly powerful! While they look very strenuous, everyone is encouraged to go along at his or her own pace.

Tae Bo brings up the healthy warrior within and helps me realize that I can handle all that needs to be handled in a life-affirming way. Meditation, yoga, and other such calming techniques are wonderful for building a sense of peace within, but for building a sense of power, Tae Bo or other exercise techniques derived from the martial arts gives us a sense of "bring it all on, World. I'm ready!" And there are many out there for every level of physical strength. A great gift, indeed!

FOR PEACE OF MIND . . . I would recommend giving a Laughing Buddha. As many of you already know, I have a number of Laughing Buddhas prominently placed throughout my office and my home. Any time I am driving myself crazy trying to control everything around me, I look at my Laughing Buddha and laugh right along with him. I let go and lighten up. The Laughing Buddha reminds me that peace and joy lie within, not "out there" somewhere. And we all need reminders! Yes, the Laughing Buddha can be a wonderful gift to those you love.

FOR LOVE . . . I would recommend writing a letter thanking your loved ones for all they have contributed to your life. And how much they mean to you. This requires us to focus on the beauty and to let go of our complaints. (For those of you who have been treated badly by people in your life, remember there is always something to thank them for. Just look for the "something" and thank them for that.)

It is such a beautiful act to let your loved ones know you love and appreciate their gifts to your life. A beautiful heart-shaped trinket could accompany the letters, but I suspect it is the words reflecting your love and thanks that they will treasure forever.

By the way, giving this gift creates a few unexpected treasures for you as well.

—It feels so good to thank people for their contributions to your life.

—As you give your gift of "thanks", it makes you realize how lucky you are to have people in your life who have given you so much.

—As others are moved by your thanks, you are reminded that you truly do make a difference to the well-being of those around you.

It is amazing how easily those two little words, THANK YOU, can make both the "Giver" and the "Getter" happy!

With that in mind, it is now my turn to send all of you a from-my-heart THANK YOU for participating in my life in so many meaningful ways. The fact that you log onto my website, read my books, listen to my tapes, and let me know I make a difference in your life means so much to me.

Like all of you, there are times when I get tired and discouraged when things are not happening as I would like them to happen . . . .and then I receive a special THANK YOU from one of you . . . whether in an e-mail, a card, a letter, a beautiful "customer review" on an internet bookstore, a hug when I give a talk, or whatever. And I am filled with resolve and strength once again. You cannot imagine the great power of your THANK YOU's. They make my heart sing.

And on that happy note, please accept my thanks, my love, and my deepest wish that your holiday season is filled with much, much joy . . . for yourself and for those to whom you give away your own very special gifts of POWER, PEACE and LOVE.

50.

Embracing the World Like a Lover

I wanted to end *Life is Huge!* with this passage from *Dare to Connect* which contains the essence of so much that I believe.

I BELIEVE THAT IT IS OUR NATURE to connect. Starting from the deepest place within our being and expanding out to our family and friends, the workplace, our community, and ultimately to our entire planet, we are naturally pulled forward to reach out and touch the entire world around us. I believe that even though our training is about competing, our Souls are about embracing. The only thing that stops us are the erroneous teachings of a Society that has lost its Spirituality.

And what do I mean by Spirituality? No, it's not about religion. Whether religious or not, a Spiritual person is one who lives from the highest part of who they are . . . the part of them that is loving, joyful, powerful and all things life-enhancing. This, in contrast, to one who lives from the lowest part of who they are . . . the part of them that is filled with a sense of fear, anger, powerlessness and all things life-destroying.

Obviously, a Society lacking in Spirituality offers no lasting solutions to the problem of alienation that envelopes it. This thought can be very depressing, that is, until we ask ourselves a key question: "Who creates Society?" The answer, of course, is "We do . . . you and I". This reality offers us much hope. It says that you and I can take hold of the reins and begin to steer our Society out of the realm of alienation and into a place that feels more like Home.

While this sounds like an impossible task, I don't believe it is. All that is required is that we begin our own personal Journey inward to our Higher Self—the best of who we are . . . and then radiate the best of who we are out to those around us, thereby playing a vital role in the transformation of Society at large.

We can begin by asking ourselves as we move through each activity of our day and as we touch the lives of those around us:

—How can I be softer and more loving here?
—How can I reach out to the people in the world around me?
—How can I radiate light in a world that sometimes looks very dark?
—How can I open my Heart and take more responsibility in healing the hurts I see around me every day of my life?

Deep, exciting, challenging and wonderful questions. As we keep asking ourselves these questions in more and more situations and (this is important!) then taking actions based on the answers we receive, we begin to drink in the good feelings that loving actions create . . .

we embark on a new kind of lifestyle which is infused with love and caring . . . and I do believe that the radiant energy that this kind of lifestyle creates spreads much, much further into the world than our mortal eyes can see.

There is little doubt that we can create connection where alienation now exists by simple acts of caring. Acts of caring can be seen as light from the Soul. I have seen this light of the Soul come forward to touch other Souls in many unexpected ways. An example:

One day as I was walking down the street in New York City, I saw half-way down the block a young tough-looking man swaggering arrogantly in and out of the crowd. I pre-judged him as someone who wouldn't give the time of day to anyone on the street, not that anyone would dare to ask!

At one point, his eye caught sight of a blind old man with a cane tottering precariously toward the curb. At once, he ran forward and headed the old man off before any damage was done. Then he took off down the street once again. After he progressed a little way, he turned back to see if the old man was keeping on a straight course. No, he was once again headed for the curb. The young man darted back and impatiently told the old man he was still going toward the curb. But to no avail. Yet again, the old man went off course.

Finally, with a nod of resignation, our tough-guy teamed up with the little old man, and this very unlikely couple proceeded nobly down the street . . . together. Magical! A moment of connection. A moment of the divine. (And an eye-opener to me about judging people by their appearance!)

How easy it is to bring Spirituality into our everyday lives. One simple act of caring and the whole world around us (and beyond) is transformed. (Yes, there is much scientific evidence that energy travels much further than our mortal eyes can see.) Everyone is touched, uplifted and comforted. It takes so little . . . just a little attention off the self, the opportunity to say to someone else, "Hi, I'm here. How can I help you on your Journey on this very strange planet?"

We can bring a quality of caring to all our human exchanges, whatever they may be. You can begin by asking yourself, "If I were really an important member of this global family, what would I be doing?" And then, proceed to do it one step at a time. You will be amazed at how much distance your loving light can cover in this step-by-step process.

There will be times when you forget how important you really are. So to help you imprint it permanently in your mind, I'd like you to repeat the following at least ten times every single day of your life from this day forth:

"Who I am is someone who has the power within to create a Heaven on earth for myself and to radiate a piece of that Heaven out to everyone whose life touches mine . . . and beyond."

Repeat it over and over again for as many days, months, or years it takes, until you fully take in its implications and begin to consciously live your life within its truth. As you begin to understand the immense power and love you hold inside, you will find an unending surge of joy, light and love that will nourish and support you all the days of your life.

© 1991 Susan Jeffers, Ph.D.

(Adapted from *Dare to Connect*)

ENDNOTES

Chapter 2
1. Frankl, Viktor. *Man's Search for Meaning.* Pocket Books, (A division of Simon and Schuster, Inc.), 1959, 1962, 1984 (First published in Austria in 1946).

Chapter 11
1. Kanin, Garson. *It Takes a Long Time to Become Young.* Berkley Publishing, 1981.

Chapter 14
1. A Steven Spielberg film, starring Liam Neeson and Ralph Fiennes, Universal Studios, 1993. Adapted from the 1982 book *Schindler's List* by Thomas Keneally.

Chapter 18
1. The "Fear-Less Series" of affirmation books and tapes (*Inner Talk for Peace of Mind, Inner Talk for a Confident Day* and *Inner Talk for a Love That Works*).

2. www.susanjeffers.com

3. Jeffers, Susan and Gradstein, Donna, *I Can Handle It!* Vermilion, London, (The Random Huse Group), 2002.

4. Jeffers, Susan. *Feel the Fear . . . And Beyond*. A Fawcett Book, (Ballantine), 1998.

Chapter 27
1. Cohen, Alan. *Joy Is My Compass*. Dolphin Communications Co., 1990.

Chapter 29
1. This information came from the U.S. Department of Health and Human Services. Child Maltreatment 1996: Reports from the States to the National Child Abuse and Neglect Data System (Washington, DC: U.S. Government Printing Office, 1998) and The National Clearinghouse on Child Abuse and Neglect Information, PO Box 1182, Washington, DC 20013-1182. I suspect similar findings would be found in all Western societies where the structure of the family is the same as the United States.

Chapter 39
1. If you want to learn how to create a self-help group, read *Dare to Connect* and *Feel the Fear . . . And Beyond*.

Chapter 42
1. Music and lyrics by Stephen Sondheim, Book by James Lapine, Starring Vanessa Williams and John McMartin.

Chapter 43
1. www.insideedge.org

Chapter 44
1. *I Can Handle It*, Vermilion London, (The Random House Group), 2002
2. *I Can Handle It, pages 140-141.*